Henry Edward Manning

The temporal mission of the Holy Ghost

Reason and revelation

Henry Edward Manning

The temporal mission of the Holy Ghost
Reason and revelation

ISBN/EAN: 9783337281588

Printed in Europe, USA, Canada, Australia, Japan

Cover: Foto ©Lupo / pixelio.de

More available books at **www.hansebooks.com**

THE
TEMPORAL MISSION
OF
THE HOLY GHOST:
OR
REASON AND REVELATION.

BY

HENRY EDWARD,
CARDINAL ARCHBISHOP OF WESTMINSTER.

Τίς οὖν ἄρα ἡ χάρις, ἢ πάντως ἡ τοῦ ἁγίου Πνεύματος χύσις ἡ ἐν ταῖς καρδίαις ἡμῶν γινομένη, κατὰ τὴν τοῦ Παύλου φωνήν . . . αὐτουργὸν ἄρα τὸ Πνεῦμα ἐν ἡμῖν, ἀληθῶς ἁγιάζον καὶ ἑνοῦν ἡμᾶς ἑαυτῷ διὰ τῆς πρὸς αὐτὸ συναφείας, θείας τε φύσεως ἀποτελοῦν κοινωνούς.
S. CYRIL. ALEX. *Thesaur. de Trin. Assert.* xxxiv.

Si dicatur: *In sanctam Ecclesiam Catholicam,* hoc est intelligendum secundum quod fides nostra refertur ad Spiritum Sanctum, qui sanctificat Ecclesiam, ut sit sensus: *Credo in Spiritum Sanctum sanctificantem Ecclesiam.*
S. THOM. *Sum. Theol.* 2ᵈᵃ 2ᵈᵃᵉ Quæs. 1. Art. 9 ad 5.

THIRD EDITION.

LONDON:
LONGMANS, GREEN, AND CO.
1877.

TO THE CONGREGATION

OF THE

OBLATES OF S. CHARLES,

IN THE

DIOCESE OF WESTMINSTER.

———◆———

Reverend and dear Fathers,

  To whom can I more fittingly dedicate the following pages than to you, with whom I have spent eight of the happiest years of my life? If the book has no worth in itself, at least it will express my affection. It was written last year under the quiet roof of S. Mary of the Angels, at a time when I had no thought of being parted from you; if, indeed, I may call that a parting which, though it suspends our daily and hourly meeting in community, unites us doubly in the bonds of mutual confidence and service. Nevertheless, though written in other days, I see no reason why it should not be published now.

Such as it may be, you will there find the result of the days which are now, I fear, not to return. S. Augustine says, 'Otium sanctum quærit charitas veritatis. Negotium justum suscipit necessitas charitatis. Quam sarcinam si nullus imponit, percipiendæ atque intuendæ vacandum est veritati.'* I cannot say that our life together had much leisure in it, but it had times of quiet and many helps, and facilities of theological reading and calm thought, which I can hardly hope for again. The 'Sarcina negotii' has been laid upon me, and I must bear my burden as I may.

You will, I hope, see in these pages nothing contrary to the spirit of our glorious Father and Patron, S. Charles, who has always seemed to me to represent in an especial way, not so much any particular doctrine of the Faith, as the Divine authority of the Church, expressed by its Councils, its Pontiffs, and its continuous living

---

* S. Aug. De Civit. Dei, lib. xix. c. 19. tom. vii. p. 563.

and infallible voice. And this appears to me the truth which the great religious confusions of the last three hundred years have completely effaced from the intelligence of the greater part of our countrymen. S. Charles would seem, therefore, to have a special mission to England and to the nineteenth century.

I hope, too, that in these pages will be found nothing inconsistent with the injunctions of our Rule, which binds us 'ad studium culturamque disciplinarum Theologicarum quæ pro consilio Sancti Caroli ad normam Tridentini Concilii exactæ maxime sint ; eoque pertineant ut Romanæ Sedis auctoritas splendescat.'[*] If we are to 'serve our generation by the will of God,' it must be by the boldest and clearest enunciation of the great principles of Divine certainty in matters of Faith, and by pointing out the relations of Faith to human knowledge, scientific and moral.

On this will depend the purity of Catholic education ; and the reconciliation of 'Faith with science and dogma with free-thought,'—problems insoluble to all who reject the infallibility of the

---

[*] Instit. Oblatorum S. Caroli, &c., p. 11.

Church, because by that rejection they destroy one of the terms of the question. On this also will depend many practical consequences of vital moment at this time: such as the relations of the Church and of the Faith to the political and social changes of this age: the limits of true and of false liberty of the intellect and the will, in individuals and in societies of men, for which the Sovereign Pontiff has lately given to us, in the Encyclical of last year, an outline and guidance worthy of the Supreme Teacher of the faithful. But it is not my object to anticipate the matter of this book, nor to do more than to point to subjects of which, I trust, if God so will, I may have time to speak hereafter.

I remember in one of the last nights when I was watching by the dying-bed of our dear and lamented Cardinal, that these thoughts, on which I had heard him so often speak with the abundance and vigour of his great mind, came with a special vividness before me, and I thanked God from my heart for having laid upon us this work through the wisdom of our great Pastor and Friend who was so soon to be taken from us. To him we owe the direction which every year more luminously shows to be the only true remedy, both intellectually and spiritually, for the evils of our time and country. I little thought at that hour that I should date these words to you from under the same roof, where everything speaks to me, all the day long, of his memory and of our loss.

Persevere, then, Reverend and dear Fathers, in the path into which he led us. The English people are fair and truthful. They are listening for a voice to guide them in the midst of their contradictory teachers. The errors of the last three hundred years are passing fast away. Preach the Holy Catholic and Roman Faith in all its truth, and in all its fulness. Speak, as none other can, with the authority of God and His infallible Church. Preach as the Apostles preached, and, as the Rule enjoins, with a 'sancta et virilis simplicitas,' with a holy and manly simplicity. Contend with men, as a loved and honoured friend has said of the Apostles, 'They argued not, but preached; and conscience did the rest.' If what I here offer you may help you, use it. If it come short, follow out the same studies and fill up what I have left imperfect.

If I had been able, as I thought, to go to Rome before publishing these pages, I should have submitted them to examination before I made them public. As it is, I can only commend them to the censure of those who can correct me if I shall have erred, and above all to the unerring judgment of the Holy See; taking S. Bernard's words as my own: 'Quæ autem dixi, absque præjudicio sane dicta sint sanius sapientis. Romanæ præsertim Ecclesiæ auctoritati atque examini totum hoc, sicut et cætera quæ ejusmodi sunt, universa refero: ipsius si quid aliter sapio, paratus judicio emendare.'*

My prayers, day by day, are offered up for you at the altar that every grace may prosper you and the Congregation of S. Charles.

Believe me, Reverend and dear Fathers,
 Always your very affectionate Servant
  in Jesus Christ,
   ✠ H. E. M.

8 York Place: July 15, 1865.

* Epist. ad Canon. Lugdun., tom i. p. 76.

CONTENTS.

INTRODUCTION.
(pp. 1–35.)

Object and method of the work. A Divine Teacher always present. Reason either a disciple or a critic. Rationalism true and false. In the former sense it signifies the use of the reason in *testing the evidence of a revelation alleged to be divine,* or in perceiving the *harmony of the Divine Revelation with the human reason.* In the latter sense defined to be *an abnormal and illegitimate use of the reason.* Divided into perfect and imperfect, or fully-developed and incipient. 1. The former assumes reason to be the *fountain* of all knowledge relating to God and to the soul, and therefore the *source, measure,* and *limit* of what is credible in the theology of natural religion, to the exclusion of all supernatural revelation. 2. The latter assumes reason to be the supreme *test* or *judge* of the intrinsic credibility of revelation admitted in the main to be supernatural. Both kinds of Rationalism are one in principle: both lower the reason. Incipient Rationalism in the Anglican Church. The Church teaches that Faith is an infused grace which elevates and perfects the reason. Object of the present work to show: 1. That to believe in Revelation is the highest act of the human reason. 2. That to believe in Revelation, whole and perfect, is the perfection of the reason. 3. That to submit to the Voice of the Holy Spirit in the Church is the absolute condition to attain a perfect knowledge of Revelation. 4. That the Divine Witness of the Holy Spirit in the Church anticipates the criticism of the human reason, and refuses to be subject to it. The four bases or motives of Faith are: 1. That it is a violation of reason not to believe in the existence of God. 2. That it is a violation of our moral sense not to believe that God has made Himself known to man. 3. That the Revelation He has given is Christianity, 4. That Christianity is Catholicism. Each of these four truths certain by its own proper evidence, and each also confirmatory of the other.

Christianity the summing up and final expression in the Person of JESUS CHRIST, of all the truths of the natural and supernatural order in Judaism and Paganism. Other religions fragmentary and local. Belief in the Holy Trinity leads to belief in Catholicism.

Three Divine Persons; three Divine offices—the Father and Creation; the Son and Redemption; the Holy Ghost and the Church. Definition of the TEMPORAL MISSION OF THE HOLY GHOST: *The sending, advent, and office of the Holy Ghost through the Incarnate Son, and after the day of Pentecost.* The *Eternal Procession* of the Holy Ghost completes the mystery of the Holy Trinity *ad intra;* the *Temporal Mission* of the Holy Ghost completes the revelation of the Holy Trinity *ad extra.*

Testimony of S. AUGUSTINE. The Author's retractation of three errors: 1. Of false rule of Faith. 2. Of false theory of unity. 3. Of false view of the position of the Roman Pontiff. Unity of the Church indivisible and singular. Passing away of the so-called reformation.

CHAPTER I.

THE RELATION OF THE HOLY GHOST TO THE CHURCH.

(pp. 36–92.)

In the Baptismal Creed the article on the Church is united to the article on the Holy Ghost, to signify that the union between the Holy Ghost and the Church is divinely constituted, indissoluble and eternal. By this union the Church is immutable in its *knowledge, discernment,* and *enunciation* of the truth. 1. Proved from HOLY SCRIPTURE, *S. John* xiv. xvi., *Eph.* iv., *Rom.* xii., 1 *Cor.* xii. 2. Proved by passages from the Fathers, S. IRENÆUS, TERTULLIAN, S. AUGUSTINE, S. GREGORY OF NAZIANZUM, S. CYRIL OF ALEXANDRIA, and S. GREGORY THE GREAT. Two conclusions follow: 1. The present dispensation that of the Holy Spirit. 2. It differs from His presence and office before the advent of JESUS CHRIST in many gifts, graces and manifestations, and principally in five ways:

I. *The Holy Ghost came before into the world by His universal operations in all mankind, but now He comes through the Incarnate Son by a special and personal presence.* Proved from II. SCRIPTURE, S. AUGUSTINE, and S. THOMAS. Explained by SUAREZ and PETAVIUS.

II. *Before the day of Pentecost the Mystical Body of Christ was not complete: the Holy Ghost came to perfect its creation and organization.* The Constitution of the Body was deferred until the Head was glorified. 1. Christ, as Head of the Church, is the fountain of all sanctity to His mystical Body. *Col.* i. 19, *Eph.* i. 22. S. GREGORY THE GREAT and S. AUGUSTINE. 2. The sanctification of the Church is effected by the gift of the Holy Ghost. *Eph.* ii. 22, *Rom.* v. 5, 1 *Cor.* iii. 16. S. ATHANASIUS and S. CYRIL OF ALEXANDRIA. 3. The Holy Ghost dwells personally and substantially in the mystical Body, which is the incorporation of those who are sanctified. 4. The members of the mystical Body who are sanctified, partake not only of the created graces, but of a substantial union with the Holy Ghost. 5. The union of the Holy Ghost with the mystical Body, though analogous to the hypostatic union, is not hypostatic; forasmuch as the human personality of the members of Christ still subsists in this substantial union. References to PETAVIUS and THOMASSINUS.

III. *The Holy Ghost came at Pentecost to constitute a union between Himself and the Mystical Body that would be absolute and indissoluble.* Before the Incarnation He wrought in the souls of men, one by one. His presence, therefore, was conditional, depending on the human will, as it is now in individuals as such; but in the Church His presence depends on the Divine will alone, and is therefore perpetual. 1. The union of the Holy Ghost with the Head of the Church, both as God and as Man, is indissoluble. 2. There will always be a mystical Body for that Divine Head, although individuals may fall from it. Three divine and eternal unions, (1.) Of the Head with the members, (2.) Of the members with each other, (3.) Of the Holy Ghost with the Body, constitute the complete organization of the Church. Its endowments are derived from the Divine Person of its Head, and the Divine Person who is its Life. It receives a communication of the perfections of the Holy Ghost. It is *imperishable,* because He is God; *indivisibly* one, because He is numerically one; *holy,* because He is the fountain of holiness; *infallible*, because He is the Truth. Its members not only *called* or *elected*, but *aggregated* or *called into one*. The Church, therefore, is a mystical *person*, not on probation, but the instrument of probation to others.

IV. *Before the Incarnation the Holy Ghost wrought invisibly: now by His Temporal Mission He has manifested His presence and His operations by the Visible Church of Jesus Christ.* 1. The Church is the evidence of the presence of the Holy Ghost among men, the *visible incorporation* of His presence: (1.) By its supernatural and worldwide *unity*. S. AUGUSTINE quoted. (2.) By its *imperishableness* in the midst of the dissolving works of man. (3.) By its *immutability* in doctrine of faith and morals. 2. The Church is the instrument of the power of the Holy Ghost: (1.) By the perpetuity and diffusion of the light of the Incarnation. (2.) By the perpetuity of sanctifying grace by means of the Seven Sacraments. 3. It manifests for various ends and at various times His *miraculous* power. 4. It is the organ of His voice.

General Summary.—From the indissoluble union of the Holy Ghost flow: 1. The three *properties* of UNITY, VISIBLENESS and PERPETUITY; 2. The three *endowments*, namely; INDEFECTIBILITY in life and duration, INFALLIBILTY in teaching, and AUTHORITY in governing; 3. The four *notes*, namely, UNITY, SANCTITY, CATHOLICITY, and APOSTOLICITY.

V. *Before the Incarnation the Holy Ghost taught and sanctified individuals, but with an intermitted exercise of His visitations; now He teaches and sanctifies the Body of the Church permanently.*

Three possibly conceivable Rules of Faith; 1. A living Judge and Teacher, or the Divine Mind declaring itself through an organ of its own creation. 2. The Scriptures interpreted by the reason of individuals. 3. Scripture and Antiquity. The two last resolvable into one, namely, the human mind judging for itself upon the evidence and contents of revelation. Its refutation. False theory of a Church once undivided and infallible and afterwards divided and fallible. S. CYPRIAN and S. BEDE quoted.

The office of the Holy Ghost as Illuminator consists in the following operations: 1. In the original revelation to the Apostles. 2. In the preservation of what was revealed. 3. In assisting the Church to conceive, with greater fulness, explicitness and clearness, the original truth in all its relations. 4. In defining that truth in words. 5. In the perpetual enunciation and propositions of the same immutable truth. *De Locis Theologicis:* (1.) Voice of the Living Church, (2.) The Holy Scriptures, (3.) Tradition, (4.) The decrees of General Councils, (5.) The definitions and decrees of Sovereign Pontiffs speaking *ex cathedrâ*, (6.) The unanimous voice of the Saints, (7.) The consent of Doctors. (8.) The voice of the Fathers, (9.) The authority of Philosophers, (10.) Human History, (11.) Natural Reason.

CHAPTER II.

THE RELATION OF THE HOLY GHOST TO THE HUMAN REASON.

(pp. 93-133.)

Two ways of treating this relation: 1. In those who do not believe, 2. In those who do believe. In the former case Reason must, by necessity, ascertain, examine, judge, and estimate the evidence of the *fact* of a revelation, its *motives* of credibility and its *nature*. In the latter case it submits as a disciple to a Divine Teacher. S. THOMAS quoted to show the office of reason in regard to revelation; 1. Faith presupposes the operations of reason, on the motives of credibility for which we believe. 2. Faith is rendered intrinsically credible by reason. 3. Faith is illustrated by reason. 4. Faith is defended by reason against the sophisms of false philosophy.

The relations of reason to revelation are principally five:

I. *Reason receives Revelation by intellectual apprehension.* Analogy of the eye and light. Knowledge of God both in Nature and Revelation a gift or infusion to man, not a discovery by logic or research. Reference to VIVA. What was revealed by our Lord and the Holy Ghost inherited and sustained by the Church.

II. *Reason propagates the truths of Revelation.* The Divine commission to the Apostles. Faith came by hearing.

III. *Reason defines the truths of Revelation divinely presented to it.* The Creeds, General Councils, Definitions, and the science of Theology.

IV. *Reason defends Revelation.* 1. *Negatively*, by showing the nullity of arguments brought against it: 2. *positively*, by demonstrating its possibility, fitness, necessity, and reality. Sketch of the history of Theology. The ancient *Apologies* of the early Fathers. The Greek and Latin Fathers. S. JOHN OF DAMASCUS, *De Orthodoxâ Fide* in the eighth century. LANFRANC and S. ANSELM in the eleventh. *Cur Deus Homo.* S. BERNARD and ABELARD. PETER LOMBARD, *Liber Sententiarum.* ALBERTUS MAGNUS, S. BONAVENTURA, S. THOMAS. *Summa Theologica.* The Dominican and Jesuit Commentators. The Council of TRENT. History of Dogma.

V. *Reason transmits Revelation by a scientific treatment and tradition.* Theology though not a science *propriè dicta*, may be truly and correctly so described. The definition of Science in Scholastic Philosophy taken from ARISTOTLE. The sense in which Theology is a Science. Opinions of S. THOMAS, CAJETAN, VASQUEZ, and GREGORY OF VALENTIA. Fourteen *General Conclusions* stated as propositions.

CHAPTER III.

THE RELATION OF THE HOLY GHOST TO THE LETTER OF SCRIPTURE.

(pp. 134–182.)

Object of this chapter to trace an outline of the history of the Doctrine of INSPIRATION.

I. In every century there have been objectors, gainsayers and unbelievers, from Cerinthus, Marcion, and Faustus the Manichæan, to Luther, Spinoza, Paine, and modern rationalists.

II. Doctrine of INSPIRATION in the Church of England. References to HOOKER, WHITBY, and Bishop BURNET. Various modern opinions. The *Essays and Reviews.*

III. The Catholic Doctrine of INSPIRATION. Five points of faith.

1. That the writings of the Prophets and Apostles are Holy Scripture. 2. That God is the Author of the Sacred Books. 3. That the Sacred Books are so many in number and are such by name. 4. That these books in their integrity are to be held as sacred and canonical. 5. That the Latin version called the Vulgate is authentic.

First period: of simple faith.—The Fathers both of the East and West extend the Inspiration of the Holy Ghost to the whole of Scripture, both to its substance and to its form. Proved from S. IRENÆUS, S. MACARIUS, S. CHRYSOSTOM, S. BASIL, S. GREGORY OF NAZIANZUM, and S. JOHN OF DAMASCUS. Also from S. AUGUSTINE, S. GREGORY THE GREAT, and S. AMBROSE.

Second Period: of analysis as to the nature and limits of Inspiration.—Two schools of opinion.
1. *Every particle and word of the Canonical books was written by the dictation of the Holy Spirit.* TOSTATUS. ESTIUS. Faculties of LOUVAIN and DOUAI, MELCHIOR CANUS, BAÑEZ, and the Dominican Theologians generally.
2. *The whole matter of Holy Scripture was written by the assistance of the Holy Spirit, but not the whole form dictated by Him.* BELLARMINE, the Jesuit Theologians, and the majority of recent writers on the subject. Opinions of Luther and Erasmus. Discussion caused by the propositions of Lessius and Hamel. P. Simon and Holden. Definition of *Inspiration, Revelation, Suggestion, and Assistance.*

Inspiration includes: 1. The impulse to put in writing the matter which God wills. 2. The suggestion of the matter to be written. 3. The assistance which excludes liability to error. *Theologia Wirceburgensis.* Statement of supposed difficulties. Reply to objections gathered from S. JEROME. In what sense the Vulgate is authentic.

Whensoever the text can be undoubtedly established, the supposition of error as to the contents of that text cannot be admitted. Wheresoever the text may be uncertain, in those parts error may be present—this would be an error of *transcription* or *translation.* 1. The Holy Scripture does not contain a revelation of the physical sciences. 2. No system of chronology is laid down in the Sacred Books. 3. Historical narratives may appear incredible and yet be true. S. AUGUSTINE quoted.

a

CHAPTER IV.

THE RELATION OF THE HOLY GHOST TO THE INTERPRETATION OF SCRIPTURE.

(pp. 183-221.)

Christianity neither derived from Scripture, nor dependent upon it. What the Incarnate Son was to the Scriptures of the Old Testament, that the Holy Ghost, *servatâ proportione*, is to the Scriptures of the New. England has hitherto preserved the belief that Christianity is a Divine Revelation, and that the Holy Scripture is an inspired Book. Fruits of the Reformation in other countries. In the Catholic Church the relations of the Holy Ghost to the interpretation of Scripture are:

1. *The Revelation of the Spirit of God was given, preached, and believed before the New Testament existed.* S. IRENÆUS quoted.

II. *This Revelation was also divinely recorded before the New Testament Scriptures were written.* 1. Upon the minds of pastors and people. 2. In the Seven Sacraments. 3. In the visible worship of the Church. 4. In the early Creeds. Table of the dates of the Books of the New Testament.

III. *The Science of God, incorporated in the Church, is the true key to the interpretation of Scripture.* The unvarying witness of the Catholic Faith contrasted with the divers interpretations of Protestant sects.

IV. *The Church is the guardian both of the Faith and of the Scriptures.* It received both from its Divine Head. It alone witnesses to both: 1. With a human and historical testimony. 2. With a divine and supernatural testimony.

V. *The Church is not only the interpretation, but the interpreter of Holy Scripture.* Refutation of the Protestant theory of private interpretation. How the Divine Scriptures become human. S. JEROME quoted. Scripture abused by heretics. S. AUGUSTINE and VINCENT OF LERINS quoted. Anecdote of HENRY III. of England and S. LOUIS of France. Answer to two accusations brought against the Church: 1. That it supersedes to so great an extent the use of Scripture in the devotions of the people; and, 2. That it enunciates its doctrines in an arbitrary and dogmatic way, regardless of the facts of Christian antiquity and history. In the Church alone the Scriptures retain their whole and perfect meaning. Examples given. The Church has a profound sense of their sacredness. Illustrations from the lives of S. PAULINUS, S. EDMUND, and S. CHARLES.

CHAPTER V.

THE RELATION OF THE HOLY GHOST TO THE DIVINE TRADITION OF THE FAITH.

(pp. 222-260.)

Christianity has been preserved pure. Analogy between the Church in Rome in the fourth century and in England in the present. Signs of the dissolution of the various forms of Protestantism. The real question between the Catholic Church and all Christian bodies separated from it—not one of *detail* but of *principle*. Charge of corruption brought against Catholic doctrines. God alone can reform His Church. The 'Unction from the Holy One' always present to preserve the Faith. Proof from 1 S. JOHN ii. drawn out in full. As a consequence of this truth it follows:

I. All the doctrines of the Church to this day are *incorrupt*.

II. They are also *incorruptible*.

III. They are also *immutable*. Change of growth different from that of decay. Sense in which the doctrines of the Church are said to *grow*; e.g. the dogmas of the Holy Trinity, of the Incarnation, of the Blessed Eucharist, and of the Immaculate Conception. In Protestantism the doctrines of Christianity have suffered the change of *decay*.

IV. The doctrines of the Church are always *primitive*. The Church ever ancient and ever new.

V. They are also *transcendent* because *divine*. In the supernatural order, Faith must come before understanding. S. AUGUSTINE quoted. *Credo quia impossibile*. The Holy Spirit is the Author and Guardian of the Tradition of Christian Truth. He diffuses the light by which it is known, and presides over the selection of the terms in which it is defined and enumerated. Objection against Dogmatism.—*The Theology of the Nineteenth Century should be moral and spiritual.* Answer to objection. Analogy of philosophical truths. Dogmatic Theology consists in the scientific arrangement of the *primary* and *secondary* orders of Christian truth. A dogma is *the intellectual conception and verbal expression of a divine truth.* Consequently it cannot essentially change. Answer to objection that Dogmatic Theology is *barren* and *lifeless.* Theology divided into Dogmatic, Moral, Ascetical, and Mystical. Their mutual relations. Use made of Catholic sources by Protestant writers. Devotions of the Church founded on its doctrines: e.g. The Blessed Sacrament, The Sacred Heart, The Passion, etc. The *Spiritual Exercises* of S. IGNATIUS. Summary and Conclusion.

THE TEMPORAL MISSION OF THE HOLY GHOST.

INTRODUCTION.

BEFORE the reader proceeds to the following pages, I wish to detain him with a few introductory words.

1. Some time ago my intention was to publish a volume of Sermons on Reason and Revelation as a sequel to those on Ecclesiastical Subjects. In the preface to that volume I expressed this purpose. But when I began to write I found it impossible to throw the matter into the form of sermons. I do not imagine that the following pages have any pretensions to the character of a treatise, or any merit beyond, as I hope, correctness and conformity to Catholic theology. But I have found it necessary

to treat the subject in a less popular form than sermons would admit, and to introduce much matter which would be out of place if addressed to any such audience as our pastoral office has to do with. I was therefore compelled to write this volume in the form of a short treatise, and though I am fully conscious of its insufficiency, nevertheless I let it go forth, hoping that it may help some who have not studied these vital questions of our times, and provoke others who have studied them to write some work worthier of the subject.

Another departure from my first intention was also forced upon me. When I began to consider the nature and relations of Reason and Revelation, I found myself compelled to consider the Author and Giver of both, and the relations in which He stands to them, and they to Him. This threw the whole subject into another form, and disposed the parts of it in another order. I found myself writing on the relations of the Divine Intelligence to the human; but as these intelligent and vital powers are personal, I was led into that which seems to me, in the last analysis, to comprehend the whole question of Divine Faith, the temporal mission of the Holy Ghost, and the relations of the Spirit of Truth to the Church, to the human reason, to the Scriptures, and to the dogma of Faith. In ascending this stream of light, I found myself in the presence of its Fountain, and I have been unable, whether it be a fault or not, to contemplate the subject in any other way. It seems to me as impossible to conceive of the relations of Reason and Revelation without including the Person and action of the Spirit of Truth, as to conceive a circle without a centre from which its rays diverge. I do not deny that by intellectual abstraction we may do so, but it would be to mutilate the diagram and the truth together.

2. Now my object, in the following pages, is to show that the reason of man has no choice but to be either the disciple or the critic of the revelation of God. The normal state of the reason is that of a disciple illuminated, elevated, guided, and unfolded to strength and perfection by the action of a Divine Teacher. The abnormal is that of a critic testing, measuring, limiting the matter of Divine revelation by his supposed discernment or intuition. The former is the true and Divine Rationalism; the latter, the false and human Rationalism.

Now as, in the following pages, the words rationalism and rationalistic occur, and always in an ill sense, it will be well to say here at the outset in what sense I use it, and why I always use it in a bad signification.

By Rationalism, then, I do not mean the use of the reason in testing the evidence of a revelation alleged to be divine.

Again, by Rationalism I do not mean the perception of the harmony of the Divine revelation with the human reason. It is no part of reason to believe that which is contrary to reason, and it is not Rationalism to reject it. As reason is a divine gift equally with revelation—the one in nature, the other in grace—discord between them is impossible, and harmony an intrinsic necessity. To recognise this harmony is a normal and vital operation of the reason under the guidance of faith; and the grace of faith elicits an eminent act of the reason, its highest and noblest exercise in the fullest expansion of its powers.

By Rationalism I always intend an abnormal and illegitimate use of the reason, as I will briefly here explain. The best way to do so will be to give a short account of the introduction and use of the term.

Professor Hahn, in his book, 'De Rationalismi, qui dicitur, vera indole, et qua cum Naturalismo contineatur ratione,' says, 'As to *Rationalism*, this word was used in the seventeenth and eighteenth centuries by those who considered reason as the *source* and *norm* of faith. Amos Comenius seems first to have used this word in 1661, and it never had a good sense. In the eighteenth century it was applied to those who were in earlier times called by the name of Naturalists.'[1]

'*Naturalism*,' as Stäudlin says, 'is distinguished from Rationalism by rejecting all and every revelation of God, especially any extraordinary one, through certain men. . . . *Supernaturalism* consists in general in the conviction that God has revealed Himself supernaturally and immediately. What is revealed might perhaps be discovered by natural methods, but either not at all, or very late, by those to whom it is revealed.'[2]

Bretschneider says that the word 'Rationalism has been confused with Naturalism since the appearance of the Kantian philosophy, and that it was introduced into theology by Reinhard and Gäbler. An accurate examination respecting these words gives the following results. The word Naturalism arose first in the sixteenth century, and was spread in the seventeenth. It was understood to mean the theory of those who allowed no other knowledge of religion except the natural, which man could shape out of his own strength, and consequently excluded all supernatural revelation.' He then goes on to say that theologians

---

[1] H. T. Rose's *State of Protestantism in Germany*, Introd. xx.
[2] Ib. xviii.

distinguish three forms of Naturalism. First, Pelagianism, which admits revelation, but denies supernatural interior grace. Secondly, a grosser kind, which denies all particular revelation, such as modern Deism. Lastly, the grossest of all, which considers the world as God, or Pantheism.[1] Upon this it is obvious to remark, that the term Rationalism has been used in Germany in various senses. It has been made to comprehend both those who reject all revelation and those who profess to receive it.[2] The latter class, while they profess to receive revelation, nevertheless receive it only so far as their critical reason accepts it. They profess to receive Christianity, but they make reason the supreme arbiter in matters of faith. 'When Christianity is presented to them, they inquire what there is in it which agrees with their assumed principles (*i.e.* of intrinsic credibility), and whatsoever does so agree they receive as true.' Others again affect to allow 'a revealing operation of God, but establish on internal proofs rather than on miracles the Divine nature of Christianity. They allow that revelation *may* contain much out of the power of reason to explain, but they say that it should assert nothing contrary to reason, but

---

[1] H. T. Rose's *State of Protestantism in Germany*, Introd. xx. xxi.
[2] Ib. xxiii.

rather what may be proved by it.' But, in fact, such divines reject the 'doctrines of the Trinity, the Atonement, the Mediation and Intercession of our Lord, Original Sin, and Justification by Faith.'

I need not prolong these quotations. They suffice to show that Rationalism has various senses, or rather various degrees; but, ultimately, it has one and the same principle, namely, that the Reason is the supreme and spontaneous source of religious knowledge. It may be therefore distinguished into the perfect and imperfect Rationalism, or into the fully-developed and the incipient Rationalism, and these may perhaps be accurately described as follows:—

1. The perfect or fully-developed Rationalism is founded upon the assumption that the reason is the sole *fountain* of all knowledge relating to God and to the soul, and to the relations of God and of the soul. This does not mean the reason of each individual, but of the human race, which elicits from its own intellectual consciousness a theology of reason, and transmits it as a tradition in the society of mankind.

The reason is therefore the *source* and the *measure* or the *limit* of what is credible in the theology of rational religion. This, necessarily, excludes all supernatural revelation.[1]

[1] Rose, *ut supra*, xxiv. xxv.

2. The imperfect, or incipient, Rationalism rests upon the assumption that the reason is the supreme *test* or *judge* of the intrinsic credibility of revelation admitted in the main to be supernatural. It is easy to see that nothing but the inconsequence of those who hold this system arrests it from resolving itself into its ultimate form of perfect Rationalism. In both the reason is the critic of revelation. In the latter, it rejects portions of revealed truth as intrinsically incredible; in the former, it rejects revelation as a whole for the same reason. The latter criticises the contents of revelation, accepting the evidence of the fact, and rejects portions; the former criticises both the contents and the evidence, and altogether rejects both.

Now, it is evident that in England we are as yet in the incipient stage of Rationalism. Materialism, Secularism, and Deism are to be found in individuals, but not yet organised as schools. Rationalism in the perfect form is also to be found in isolated minds; but the incipient, or semi-Rationalism, has already established itself in a school of able, cultivated, and respectable men. I need not name the writers of whom Dr. Williams, Mr. Wilson, and Dr. Colenso are the most advanced examples. In this school most of the followers and disciples of the late Dr. Arnold are to be classed. It does not surprise me to see the rapid and consistent spread of these opinions; for ever since by the mercy of God I came to see the principle of divine faith, by which the human reason becomes the disciple of a Divine Teacher, I have seen, with the clearness of a self-evident truth, that the whole of the Anglican reformation and system is based upon the inconsequent theory which I have designated as incipient Rationalism. It admits revelation, but it constitutes the reason as the judge by critical inquiry of the contents of that revelation, of the interpretation of Scripture, and of the witness of antiquity.

The Church teaches that faith is an infused grace which elevates and perfects the reason; but as rationalists allege that faith detracts from the perfection of reason, my object will be to show:

1. That to believe in revelation is the highest act of the human reason.

2. That to believe in revelation, whole and perfect, is the perfection of the reason.

3. That to submit to the Voice of the Holy Spirit in the Church is the absolute condition to attain a perfect knowledge of revelation.

4. That the Divine witness of the Holy Spirit in the Church anticipates the criticism of the human reason, and refuses to be subject to it.

Lest anyone should imagine that in these propositions I limit the activity and office of the human reason in matters of faith, I will add also the following propositions:—

1. It would be a violation of reason in the highest degree not to believe that there is a God. To believe that this visible world is either eternal or self-created, besides all other intrinsic absurdities in the hypothesis, would simply affirm the world to be God in the same breath that we deny His existence. It would be a gross and stupid conception of an eternal and self-existent being; for to believe it self-created is a stupidity which exceeds even the stupidity of atheism. But if the world were neither eternal nor self-created, it was made; and, if made, it had a maker. Cavil as a man will, there is no escape from this necessity. To deny it is not to reason, but to violate reason; and to be rationalists, by going contrary to reason.

2. Secondly, it would be a violation of the moral sense, which is still reason judging of the relations between my Maker and myself, not to believe that He has given to me the means of knowing Him. The consciousness of what I am gives me the law by which to conceive of One higher and better than I am. If I am an intelligent and moral being, and if my dignity and my perfection consist in the perfection of my

reason and of my will, then I cannot conceive of a Being higher and better than myself, except as One who has, in a higher degree, those things which are the best and highest in myself. But my intelligent and moral nature, and the right exercise and action of its powers, is the highest and best that is in me. I know it to exceed all the other excellences which are in me. It exceeds, too, all the perfections of other creatures to whom gifts of strength and instinct have been given, without reason and the moral will.

I am certain, therefore, that my Creator is higher than I am in that which is highest in me, and therefore I know Him to be a perfect intelligence and a perfect will, and these include all the perfections of wisdom and goodness. I say then it would violate the moral sense to believe that such a Being has created me capable of knowing and of loving Him—capable of happiness and of misery, of good and of evil, and that He has never given to me the means of knowing Him, never spoken, never broken the eternal silence by a sign of His love to me, on which depend both my perfection and my happiness.

Now, it is certain, by the voice of all mankind, that God speaks to us through His works—that He whispers to us through our natural conscience—that He attracts us to Him by instincts, and desires, and aspirations after a happiness higher than sense, and more enduring, more changeless, than this mortal life. God speaks to me articulately in the stirring life of nature and the silence of our own being. What is all this but a spiritual action of the intelligence, and the will of God upon the intelligence, and will of man? and what is this but a Divine inspiration? Critically and specifically distinct as inspiration and revelation in their strict and theological sense are from this inward operation of the Divine mind upon mankind, yet generically and in the last analysis it is God speaking to man, God illuminating man to know Him, and drawing man to love Him. The inspiration and revelation granted to patriarchs, prophets, apostles, seers, and saints, are of a supernatural order, in which the lights of nature mingle and are elevated by the supernatural and divine. These manifestations of Himself to men are bestowed upon us out of the intrinsic perfections of His own Divine attributes. He created us as objects whereon to exercise His benevolence. His love and His goodness are the fountains of the light of nature. His image, in which He has created us, by its own instincts turns to Him with the rational and moral confidence that if we feel after Him we shall find Him. And His love and His goodness are such, that our yearnings for a knowledge of Him are satisfied not only by the light of nature, but through His grace by the supernatural revelation of Himself.

3. Thirdly, I am certain, with a certainty which is higher than any other in the order of moral convictions, that if there be a revelation of God to man, that revelation is Christianity. The reason of this belief is, that I find in Christianity the highest and purest truth, on the highest and purest matter of which the human intelligence is capable ; that is to say, the purest Theism or knowledge of God, the purest anthropology or science of man, and the purest morality, including the moral conduct of God towards man, and the moral action of man towards God. These three elements constitute the highest knowledge of which man is capable, and these three are to be found in their highest and purest form in Christianity alone. All the fragments or gleams of original truth which lingered yet in the religions and philosophies of the world are contained, elevated, and perfected in the doctrine of the Holy Trinity, and of the Divine perfections revealed in it; in the doctrine of the Incarnation, and the perfections of our manhood manifested in the person of Jesus Christ ; and in the Sermon on the Mount, interpreted by the example of Him who spoke it. In these three

revelations of the Divine and human natures, God has made Himself known to us, as the object of our love and worship, the pattern of our imitation, and the source of our eternal bliss. Now no other pretended revelation, no other known religion, so much as approximates to the truth and purity of the Christian faith. They are visibly true and pure only so far as they contain germs of it. They are visibly impure and false wheresoever they depart from it. They bear a twofold testimony to its perfection, both where they agree and where they disagree with it. And that which is true of Christianity, viewed objectively in itself, is also visibly true when viewed subjectively in its history. Christianity has created Christendom; and Christendom is the manifestation of all that is highest, purest, noblest, most God-like in the history of mankind. Christianity has borne the first-fruits of the human race.

4. Fourthly, Christianity, in its perfection and its purity, unmutilated, and full in its orb and circumference, is Catholicism. All other forms of Christianity are fragmentary. The revelation given first by Jesus Christ, and finally expanded to its perfect outline by the illumination of the day of Pentecost, was spread throughout the world. It took possession of all nations, as the dayspring takes possession of the

face of the earth, rising and expanding steadily and irresistibly. So the knowledge of God and of His Christ filled the world. And the words of the prophet were fulfilled, 'The idols shall be utterly destroyed;'[1] not with the axe and the hammer only, but by a mightier weapon. 'Are not my words as a fire, and as a hammer that breaketh the rock in pieces?'[2] Idolatry was swept from the face of the world by the inundation of the light of the knowledge of the true God. 'The earth shall be filled, that men may know the glory of the Lord, as waters covering the sea.'[3] The unity and universality of Christianity, and of the Church in which it was divinely incorporated, and of Christendom, which the Church has created, exclude and convict as new, fragmentary, and false, all forms of Christianity which are separate and local.

Now these four truths, as I take leave to call them,—first, that it is a violation of reason not to believe in the existence of God; secondly, that it is a violation of our moral sense not to believe that God has made Himself known to man; thirdly, that the revelation He has given is Christianity; and, fourthly, that Christianity is Catholicism—these four constitute a proof the certainty of which exceeds that of any other moral truth I know. It is not a chain of probabilities,

---

[1] Isaias ii. 18.   [2] Jer. xxiii. 29.   [3] Hab. ii. 14.

depending the one upon the other, but each one morally certain in itself. It is not a chain hanging by a link painted upon the wall, as a great philosophical writer of the day well describes the sciences which depend upon an hypothesis.[1] These four truths, considered in the natural order alone, rest upon the reason and the conscience, upon the collective testimony of the highest and purest intelligences, and upon the maximum of evidence in human history. The intellectual system of the world bears its witness to them; the concurrent testimony of the most elevated races of mankind confirms them. They are not four links of an imaginary chain, but the four cornerstones of truth. 'Sapientia ædificavit sibi domum.' And the house which the wisdom of God has built to dwell in is the cultivated intellect, or reason of the mystical body, incorporated and manifested to the world in the Visible Church. This wisdom of God has its base upon nature, which is the work of God, and its apex in the Incarnation, which is the manifestation of God. The order of nature is pervaded with primary truths which are known to the natural reason, and are axioms in the intelligence of mankind. Such, I affirm, without fear of Atheists, or Secularists, or Positivists, are the existence of God, His moral

[1] Whewell's *History of the Inductive Sciences*, vol. i. p. 16.

perfections, the moral nature of man, the dictates of conscience, the freedom of the will. On these descended other truths from the Father of Lights as He saw fit to reveal them in measure and in season, according to the successions of time ordained in the Divine purpose.

The revelations of the Patriarchs elevated and enlarged the sphere of light in the intelligence of men by their deeper, purer, and clearer insight into the Divine mind, character, and conduct in the world. The revelation to Moses and to the Prophets raised still higher the fabric of light, which was always ascending towards the fuller revelation of God yet to come. But in all these accessions and unfoldings of the light of God, truth remained still one, harmonious, indivisible; a structure in perfect symmetry, the finite but true reflex of truth as it reposes in the Divine Intelligence.

What is Christianity but the summing up and final expression of all the truths of the natural and supernatural order in the Person of Jesus Christ? God has made Him to be the ἀνακεφαλαίωσις, or recapitulation, of all the Theism, and of all the truths relating to the nature of man and of the moral law, which were already found throughout the world; and has set these truths in their place and proportion in the full revelation of 'the truth as it is in Jesus.' S. Paul compares the Incarnation to the Divine action, whereby the light was created on the first day. 'God, who commanded the light to shine out of darkness, hath shined in our hearts, to give the light of the knowledge of the glory of God in the face of Jesus Christ.'[1]

And here, perhaps, I may repeat the words in which I expressed the same truth some twenty years ago.

'By the unity of doctrine or faith the Church has taken up all philosophies, and consolidated them in one. Whether by the momentum of an original revelation, or by the continual guidance of a heavenly teaching, or by the natural convergence of the reason of man towards the unseen realities of truth, it is certain that all thoughtful and purer minds were gazing one way. As the fulness of time drew on, their eyes were more and more intently fixed on one point in the horizon, "more than they that watch for the morning;" and all the lights of this fallen world were bent towards one central region, in which at last they met and kindled. The one Faith was the focus of all philosophies, in which they were fused, purified, and blended. The eternity, the uncreated substance,

[1] 2 Cor. iv. 6.

the infinity of goodness, wisdom, and power, the transcendent majesty, the true personality, and the moral providence of the One supreme Maker and Ruler of the world was affirmed from heaven. The scattered truths which had wandered up and down the earth, and had been in part adored, and in part held in unrighteousness, were now elected and called home, and as it were regenerated, and gathered into one blessed company, and glorified once more as the witnesses of the Eternal.

'God was manifested as the life of the world, and yet not so as to be one with the world; but as distinct, yet filling all things. God was manifested as the source of life to man. The affinity of the soul of man to God was revealed; and the actual participation of man, through the gift of grace, in the Divine nature, and yet not so as to extinguish the distinct and immortal being of each individual soul.

'In thus taking up into itself all the scattered family of truth, the one Faith abolished all the intermingling falsehoods of four thousand years. Therefore it follows, as a just corollary, that in affirming the unity and the sovereignty of God, it annihilated the whole system of many subordinate deities. It declared absolutely that there is no God but one; that all created being is generically distinct, and has in it no Divine prerogative. It taught mankind that the wisest and the best of earth pass not the bounds of man's nature; that the passions and energies of mankind are, by God's ordinance, parts of man's own being; that they are not his lords, but themselves subject to his control; that the powers of nature are no gods, but the pressures of the one Almighty hand; and that the visible works of God are fellow-creatures with man, and put under his feet.' [1]

To say that Christianity is Catholicism, and Catholicism is Christianity, is to utter a truism. There was but One Truth, the same in all the world, until the perverse will and the perverted intellect of man broke off fragments from the great whole, and detained them in combination with error, 'holding the truth in injustice'—that is, imprisoned in bondage to human falsehood, and turned against the Revelation of God. There cannot be two Christianities, neither can a fragment be mistaken for the whole. The mountain has filled the whole earth, and the drift and detritus which fall from it cannot be taken, by any illusion, to be the mountain. The unity of Christianity is its identity with its original, and its identity in all the world. It is one and the same everywhere,

[1] *The Unity of the Church*, pp. 205, 206.

and therefore it is universal. The unity of Christianity is related to its universality, as theologians say of God, who is One not so much by number as by His immensity, which pervades eternity and excludes all other. So it may be said there is one truth which pervades the rational creation in various degrees from the first lights of nature, which lie upon the circumference, to the full illumination of the Incarnation of God, which reigns in its centre; and this divine order and hierarchy of truth excludes all other, and is both the reflex and the reality of the Truth which inhabits the Divine Intelligence. When then I say Catholicism, I mean perfect Christianity, undiminished, full-orbed, illuminating all nations, as S. Irenæus says, like the sun, one and the same in every place.[1] It seems to me that no man can believe the doctrine of the Holy Trinity in its fulness and perfection without in the end believing in Catholicism. For in the doctrine of the Holy Trinity are revealed to us Three Persons and three offices—the Father and Creation; the Son and Redemption; the Holy Ghost and the Church. Whosoever believes in these three Divine Works, holds implicitly the indivisible unity and the perpetual infallibility of the Church. But into this,

---

[1] S. Iren. *Contra Hæret.* lib. i. cap. x. sect. 2.

as it will be the subject of the first of the following chapters, I shall not enter now.

I will make only one remark upon it in explanation of the title of this volume. By the Temporal Mission of the Holy Ghost, Catholic theologians understand the sending, advent, and office of the Holy Ghost through the Incarnate Son, and after the day of Pentecost. This is altogether distinct from His Eternal Procession and Spiration from the Father and the Son. Now, it is remarkable that the schismatical Greeks, in order to justify their rejection of the *Filioque*, interpret the passages of the Scriptures and of the Fathers in which the Holy Ghost is declared to proceed or to be sent from the Father and the Son, of His Temporal Mission into the world. On the other hand, in these last centuries, those who have rejected the perpetual office of the Holy Ghost in the Church by rejecting its perpetual infallibility, interpret the same passages, not of the Temporal Mission, but of the Eternal Procession.

The Catholic theology, with the divine tradition of faith which governs its conceptions and definitions, propounds to us both the Eternal Procession and the Temporal Mission of the Holy Ghost, from the Father and the Son—the one in eternity, the other in time; the eternal completing the mystery of the Holy

Trinity *ad intra*, the temporal completing the revelation of the Holy Trinity *ad extra*.

In commenting on the sin against the Holy Ghost, S. Augustine says: 'And for this cause both the Jews and such heretics, whatsoever they be, who believe in the Holy Ghost, but deny His presence in the body of Christ—that is, in His only Church, which is no other than the Church, one and Catholic—without doubt are like the Pharisees who, at that day, though they acknowledged the existence of the Holy Spirit, yet denied that He was in the Christ.' He then argues as follows: 'For to Him [the Spirit] belongs the fellowship by which we are made the one body of the only Son of God; . . . wherefore,' he says again, 'whosoever hath not the spirit of Christ, he is none of His. For, to whom in the Trinity should properly belong the communion of this fellowship but to that Spirit who is common to the Father and the Son? That they who are separated from the Church have not this Spirit, the Apostle Jude openly declared.' In these passages S. Augustine distinctly affirms that, to deny the office of the Holy Ghost in the Church, is to deny a part of the doctrine of the Trinity. So again, speaking of the absolution of sin, S. Augustine ascribes it to the operation of the Three Persons. 'For the Holy Ghost dwells in no one without the Father and the Son; nor the Son without the Father and the Holy Ghost; nor without them the Father. For their indwelling is inseparable whose operation is inseparable. . . . But, as I have already often said, the remission of sins, whereby the kingdom of the spirit divided against himself is overthrown and cast out—and, therefore, the fellowship of the unity of the Church of God, out of which the remission of sins is not given—is the proper office of the Holy Ghost, the Father and the Son co-operating; for the Holy Ghost Himself is the fellowship of the Father and the Son. . . . Whosoever therefore is guilty of impenitence against the Spirit, in whom the unity and fellowship of the communion of the Church is held together, it shall never be forgiven him, because he hath closed against himself the way of remission, and shall justly be condemned with the spirit who is divided against himself, being also divided against the Holy Ghost, who, against Himself, is not divided. . . . And, therefore, all congregations, or rather dispersions, which call themselves churches of Christ, and are divided and contrary among themselves, and to the congregation of unity which is His true Church, are enemies: nor because they seem to have His name, do they therefore belong to His congregation. They would indeed belong to it if the

Holy Ghost, in whom this congregation is associated together, were divided against Himself. But, because this is not so (for he who is not with Christ is against Him, and he who gathers not with Him scatters), therefore, all sin and all blasphemy shall be remitted unto men in this congregation, which Christ gathers together in the Holy Ghost, and not in the spirit which is divided against himself.'[1]

[1] 'Ac per hoc et Judæi et quicumque hæretici Spiritum Sanctum confitentur, sed eum negant esse in Christi corpore, quod est unica ejus Ecclesia, non utique nisi una catholica, procul dubio similes sunt Pharisæis, qui tunc etiamsi esse Spiritum Sanctum fatebantur, negabant tamen eum esse in Christo. . . . . . Ad ipsum enim pertinet societas, qua efficimur unum corpus unici Filii Dei. . . . . Unde item dicit, Quisquis autem Spiritum Christi non habet, hic non est ejus. Ad quem ergo in Trinitate proprie pertineret hujus communio societatis, nisi ad eum Spiritum qui est Patri Filioque communis? Hunc Spiritum quòd illi non habeant, qui sunt ab Ecclesia segregati, Judas apostolus apertissimè declaravit. Neque enim habitat in quoquam Spiritus Sanctus nisi Patre et Filio: sicut nec Filius sine Patre et Spiritu Sancto, nec sine illis Pater. Inseparabilis quippe est habitatio, quorum est inseparabilis operatio. . . . . Sed ut jam non semel diximus, ideo remissio peccatorum, qua in se divisi spiritûs evertitur et expellitur regnum, ideo societas unitatis Ecclesiæ Dei, extra quam non sit ista remissio peccatorum, tamquam proprium est opus Spiritus Sancti, Patre sane et Filio cooperantibus, quia societas est quodam modo Patris et Filii ipse Spiritus Sanctus. . . . . Quisquis igitur reus fuerit impœnitentiæ contra Spiritum, in quo unitas et societas communionis congregatur Ecclesiæ, nunquam illi remittetur: quia hoc sibi clausit, ubi remittitur: et meritò damnabitur cum spiritu qui in se ipsum divisus est divisus et ipse contra Spiritum Sanctum qui in se ipsum divisus non est. . . . Et propterea omnes congregationes, vel potius dispersiones, quæ se Christi Ecclesias appellant, et sunt inter se divisæ atque

Like as in the old world the divine tradition of the knowledge of God was encompassed by corrupt and fragmentary religions, so the divine tradition of the faith is encompassed by fragmentary Christianities and fragmentary churches. The belief in the unity of God, before the Incarnation, was broken up into the polytheisms of Egypt, Greece, and Rome. Since the Incarnation this cannot be. The illumination of the Word made flesh renders impossible all polytheism and idolatry. The unity and the spirituality of the eternal God are now axioms of the human reason. But, as S. Augustine profoundly observes, the analogy still holds between the errors of the old creation and of the new. Satan, as he says, 'can no longer divide the true God, nor bring in among us false gods, therefore he has sent strifes among Christians. Because he could not fabricate many gods, therefore he has multiplied sects, and sown errors, and set up heresies.'[1]

contrariæ, et unitatis congregationi, quæ vera est Ecclesia ejus, inimicæ, non quia videntur ejus habere nomen, idcirco pertinent ad ejus congregationem. Pertinerent autem, si Spiritus Sanctus, in quo consociatur hæc congregatio, adversùm se ipsum divisus esset. Hoc autem quia non est; (qui enim non est cum Christo, contra ipsum est; et qui cum illo non congregat, spargit :) ideo peccatum omne atque omnis blasphemia dimittetur hominibus in hac congregatione, quam in Spiritu Sancto, et non adversùs se ipsum diviso, congregat Christus.' —S. Aug. Sermo lxxi., in Matt. xii., tom. v. pp. 386, 398, 401, 403.

[1] 'Unum Deum nobis dividere non potest. Falsos deos, nobis

And here I desire to fulfil a duty which I have always hoped one day to discharge; but I have hitherto been withheld by a fear lest I should seem to ascribe importance to anything I may have ever said,—I mean, to make a formal retractation of certain errors published by me when I was out of the light of the Catholic faith, and knew no better. I do not hereby imagine that anything I may have written carries with it any authority. But an error is a denial of the truth, and we owe a reparation to the truth; for the Truth is not an abstraction, but a Divine Person. I desire therefore to undo, as far as I may, the errors into which I unconsciously fell. They are chiefly three; and these three are the only formal oppositions I can remember to have made against the Catholic Church. They were made, I believe, temperately and soberly, with no heat or passion—without, I trust, a word of invective.

1. First, in the year 1838, I published a small work on 'The Rule of Faith,' in which, following with implicit confidence the language of the chief Anglican divines, I erroneously maintained that the old and true rule of faith is Scripture and antiquity, and I

supponere non potest.' . . . 'Lites immisit inter Christianos quia multos deos non potest fabricare: sectas multiplicavit, errores seminavit, hæreses instituit.'

rejected as new and untenable two other rules of faith,—first, the private judgment of the individual; and, secondly, the interpretations of the living Church.

2. Secondly, in 1841, I published a book on the 'Unity of the Church,' in which I maintained it to be one, visible, and organised, descending by succession from the beginning by the spiritual fertility of the hierarchy. But while I thought that the unity of the Church is organic and moral—that the organic unity consists in succession, hierarchy, and valid sacraments, and the moral in the communion of charity among all the members of particular churches, and all the churches of the Catholic unity, I erroneously thought that this moral unity might be permanently suspended, and even lost, while the organic unity remained intact, and that unity of communion belongs only to the perfection, not to the intrinsic essence of the Church.

3. Thirdly, in a sermon preached before the University of Oxford on November 5, 1843, speaking of the conflicts between the Holy See and the Crown of England, I used the words: 'It would seem to be the will of heaven that the dominion of the Roman Pontificate may never be again set up in this Church and realm.'

Now I feel that I owe a reparation to the truth for

these three errors. Beyond these, I am not aware that, for any published statements, I have any reparations to make. And I feel that, as the statements were not declamations, but reasoned propositions, so ought the refutation to be likewise.

The whole of the following work will, I hope, be a clear and reasoned retractation of those errors, so that I need now do no more than express, in the fewest words, what it was which led me in 1851 to revoke the statements I had made in 1841 and 1838.

It was, in one word, the subject of this volume, the Temporal Mission of the Holy Ghost. As soon as I perceived the Divine fact that the Holy Spirit of God has united Himself indissolubly to the mystical body, or Church of Jesus Christ, I saw at once that the interpretations or doctrines of the living Church are true because Divine, and that the voice of the living Church in all ages is the sole rule of faith, and infallible, because it is the voice of a Divine Person. I then saw that all appeals to Scripture alone, or to Scripture and antiquity, whether by individuals or by local churches, are no more than appeals from the divine voice of the living Church, and therefore essentially rationalistic. I perceived that I had imposed upon myself by speaking of three rules of faith ; that the only question is between two judges—the individual proceeding by critical reason, or the Church proceeding by a perpetual Divine assistance. But as I shall have to touch upon this in the first chapter, I dismiss it now.

As to the second point, the unity of the Church, I had not understood from whence the principle of unity is derived. It had seemed to be a constitutional law, springing from external organisation, highly beneficial, but not a vital necessity to the Church. I seemed to trace the visible Church to its Founder and His apostles as a venerable and world-wide institution, the channel of grace, the witness for God, and the instrument of the discipline and probation to men.

I had not as yet perceived that the unity of the Church is the external expression of the intrinsic and necessary law of its existence; that it flows from the unity of its Head, of its Life, of its mind, and of its will; or, in other words, from the unity of the Person of the Incarnate Son, who reigns in it, and of the Holy Ghost, who organises it by His inhabitation, sustains it by His presence, and speaks through it by His voice. The external unity, therefore, is not the cause but the effect of a vital law, which informs and governs the organisation of the Mystical Body, springing from within, and manifesting itself without, like as the animation and development of the body of a man, which springs from a vital principle, one and indivisible in its operations and its essence. All this escaped me while my eyes were holden in the way of twilight where I had been born. The more I read of Anglican writers upon the Church, such as Hooker, Field, Bilson, Taylor, Barrow, the more confused all seemed to become. The air grew thick around me. When from them I came to the Fathers, the preconceived modes of interpretation floated between me and the page. The well-known words of S. Cyprian, 'Unus Deus, unus Christus, una Ecclesia,' read to me 'One God, one Christ, one Church,' of many branches, many streams, many rays; one, therefore, in the trunk, the fountain, and the source, but not one by a continuous and coherent expansion and identity. I seemed to see the old dream of organic unity surviving where moral unity is lost. I failed to see that in this I was ascribing to God a numerical unity, to Christ a numerical unity, to the Church a numerical plurality; that I was playing fast and loose, using the word One in two senses; that while I confessed that God is one to the exclusion of plurality and division, and that Christ is one to the exclusion of plurality and division, I was affirming the Church to be one, including division and plurality, and that in the same breath, and by the same syllables. Nothing but a life-long illusion, which clouds the reason by the subtleties of controversy, could have held me so long in such a bondage. But nothing, I believe, would ever have set me free if I had not begun to study the question from a higher point—that is in its fountain—namely, the Mission and Office of the Holy Ghost. When I had once apprehended this primary truth, both Scripture and the Fathers seemed to stand out from the page with a new light, self-evident and inevitable. I then, for the first time, saw a truth of surpassing moment, which for my whole life had escaped me; namely, that One means One and no more. The unity of God, and of Christ, and of the Church is predicated univocally, not ambiguously. God is one in Nature, Christ one in Person, the Church one in organisation and singularity of subsistence, depending on its Head, who is One, and animated by the Holy Ghost, who is likewise One, the principle of union to the members, who constitute the one body by the intrinsic unity of its life. I could then understand why S. Cyprian not only likens the Unity of the Church to the seamless robe of Jesus, but also the weaving of that robe to the formation of the Church, which, he says, is woven *desuper*, 'from the top throughout,'[1]

[1] 'Unitatem illa portabat de superiore parte venientem, id est de

by heavenly Sacraments; that is, its unity descends from its Head, who impresses upon His mystical body the same law of visible and indivisible unity which constitutes the perfection of His natural body.

Such, then, is a brief statement of the reasons why, though I still believe the Book on 'the Unity of the Church' to be in the main sound and true in what relates to the visibleness and organisation of the Church, I must retract all that relates to the loss of moral unity or communion.

Nevertheless, for an adequate expression of my reasons, I must refer the reader to the following pages.

Lastly: as to the Pontificate of the Vicar of Jesus Christ, this is neither the time nor the place to enter into the subject. I may say, however, in a word, that the point last spoken of prescribes a truer belief in the office of the Head of the Church on earth. The Primacy of honour, but 'not of jurisdiction,' among a plurality of divided Churches, is an illusion which disappears when the true and divine unity of the kingdom which cannot be divided against itself rises into view. I saw in this the twofold relation of the

cœlo et a patre venientem, quæ ab accipiente ac possidente scindi omnino non poterat, sed totam simul et solidam firmitatem insepurabiliter obtinebat.'—S. Cyp. *De Unit. Eccles., Opp.* p. 196. Ed. Baluz.

visible Head of the Church, the one to the whole Body upon earth, the other to the Divine Head, whose vicar and representative he is. A new history of Christendom then unrolled itself before me, not that of our Lord as written by the Jews, but by His own Evangelists. I understood, what I never saw before, the meaning of Supreme Pontiff, and of Vicar of Jesus Christ. I acknowledge, therefore, that in 1843 I spoke rashly, or rather ignorantly in unbelief. But into this I cannot further enter now. I may refer to a volume on the 'Temporal Power of the Pope' as expressing more fully that which I did not so much as see afar off when I uttered the words which I hereby retract.

All things around us tell of one of those periods which come, from time to time, upon the Church and the bodies which surround it. Three hundred years have revealed at length the intrinsic anarchy and rationalism of the so-called Reformation. It is passing away before our eyes. The men of to-day reluctantly and unconsciously are undoing what their fathers did—justifying the Church of God by their unwilling testimony. The followers of human guides are disbanding and dispersing on every side; some further and further from the Light, deeper into the land 'ubi umbra mortis et nullus ordo;' others are turning back towards the illumination which hangs over the world in the Church of God. They are wayfaring painfully and in fear towards the east, meeting the dayspring which is rising upon them, journeying into the sun, which is as the light of seven days, the Person of the Spirit in the Church of Jesus Christ.

But it is time to make an end. With these few words of introduction, therefore, I will leave the subject, with the prayer that the same Holy Spirit of Truth, Who has brought me out of darkness into the light of Divine Faith, may likewise reveal to others His perpetual office, as the Divine and Infallible Teacher among men.

CHAPTER I.

THE RELATION OF THE HOLY GHOST TO THE CHURCH.

In this chapter my purpose is to show the relation of the Holy Spirit to the Church or Mystical Body of Jesus Christ. It is not by accident, or by mere order of enumeration, that in the Baptismal Creed we say, 'I believe in the Holy Ghost, the Holy Catholic Church.' These two articles are united because the Holy Spirit is united with the Mystical Body. And this union is divinely constituted, indissoluble, eternal, the source of supernatural endowments to the Church which can never be absent from it, or suspended in their operation. The Church of all ages, and of all times, is immutable in its *knowledge, discernment,* and *enunciation* of the truth; and that in virtue of its indissoluble union with the Holy Ghost, and of His perpetual teaching by its living voice, not only from council to council, and from age to age, with an intermittent and broken utterance, but always, and at all times, by its continuous enunciation of the Faith, as well as by its authoritative dogmatic decrees.

In order to show that in what follows I am but repeating the language of the Scriptures, Fathers, and Theologians, I will begin by quotations, and afterwards draw out certain conclusions from them.

I. And first, the testimonies from Scripture, which, being familiar to all, shall be recited as briefly as possible.

Our Lord promised that His departure should be followed by the advent of a Person like Himself—another Paraclete—the Spirit of Truth, who proceedeth from the Father: 'I will ask the Father, and He shall give you another Paraclete, that He may abide with you for ever. The Spirit of Truth, whom the world cannot receive, because it seeth Him not, nor knoweth Him: but you shall know Him; because He shall abide with you, and shall be in you.'[1]

'The Paraclete—the Holy Ghost—whom the Father will send in My name, He will teach you all things, and bring all things to your mind, whatsoever I shall have said to you.'[2]

'It is expedient for you that I go: for if I go not, the Paraclete will not come to you; but if I go, I will send Him to you.'[3]

---

[1] S. John xiv. 16, 17.   [2] Ib. 26.   [3] Ib. xvi. 7.

'When He, the Spirit of Truth, is come, He will teach you all truth. For He shall not speak of Himself; but what things soever He shall hear, He shall speak; and the things that are to come He shall shew you. He shall glorify Me; because He shall receive of Mine, and shall shew it to you. All things whatsoever the Father hath, are Mine. Therefore I said, He shall receive of Mine, and shew it to you.'[1]

The fulfilment of this promise ten days after the Ascension, was accomplished on the day of Pentecost by the personal Advent of the Holy Ghost, to abide for ever as the Guide and Teacher of the faithful, in the name and stead of the Incarnate Son. I forbear to quote the second chapter of the book of Acts, in which this divine fact is not only recorded but declared by the Holy Spirit Himself.

S. Paul has traced out the events and succession in this divine order, connecting them with the creation and organisation of the Church, where he says, 'One body and one spirit: as you are called in one hope of your calling. One Lord, one faith, one baptism. One God and Father of all, who is above all and through all, and in us all. But to every one of us is given grace according to the measure of the giving of Christ. Wherefore He saith, "Ascending on high

[1] S. John xvi. 13-16.

He led captivity captive; He gave gifts to men." Now, that He ascended, what is it, but because He also descended first into the lower parts of the earth? He that descended is the same also that ascended above all the heavens, that He might fill all things. And He gave some apostles, and some prophets, and other some evangelists, and other some pastors and doctors. For the perfection of the saints, for the work of the ministry, for the edifying of the body of Christ; until we all meet into the unity of faith, and of the knowledge of the Son of God, unto a perfect man, unto the measure of the age of the fulness of Christ: that henceforth we be no more children tossed to and fro, and carried about with every wind of doctrine by the wickedness of men, by cunning craftiness, by which they lie in wait to deceive. But doing the truth in charity, we may in all things grow up in Him who is the Head, even Christ; from Whom the whole body, being compacted and fitly joined together, by what every joint supplieth, according to the operation of the measure of every part, maketh increase of the body unto the edifying of itself in charity.'[1]

The same delineation of the Church as the Mystical Body runs through the epistles to the Romans and

[1] Ephes. iv. 4-16.

the Corinthians. 'For as in one body we have many members, but all members have not the same office; so we being many are one body in Christ, and every one members one of another.'[1]

Again to the Corinthians, after enumerating with great particularity the gifts and operations of the Holy Ghost he adds, that 'All these things one and the same Spirit worketh, dividing to every one according as he will. For as the body is one and hath many members; and all the members of the body, whereas they are many, yet are one body; so also is Christ. For in one Spirit were we all baptized into one body, whether Jews or Gentiles, whether bond or free; and in one Spirit we have all been made to drink. For the body also is not one member, but many. . . . Now you are the body of Christ, and members of member.'[2]

I will quote only one other passage. 'According to the operation of the might of His power, which He wrought in Christ, raising Him up from the dead, and setting Him on His right hand in the heavenly places, above all principality and power, and virtue and dominion, and every name that is named, not only in this world, but also in that which is to come. And hath subjected all things under His feet; and

---

[1] Rom. xii. 4, 5.   [2] 1 Cor. xii. 11, 12, 13, 14, 27.

hath made Him head over all the Church, which is His body, and the fulness of Him, who is filled all in all.'[1]

In these passages we have the interpretation of S. John's words: 'As yet the Spirit was not given, because Jesus was not yet glorified.'[2]

The Ascension—that is, the departure of the Second Person of the Holy Trinity—was hereby declared to be the condition ordained of God for the advent and perpetual presence of the Third. 'And the coming of the Holy Ghost is likewise declared to be the condition of the creation, quickening, and organisation of the mystical body, which is the Church of Jesus Christ.

II. Next, for the teaching of the Fathers; and first, S. Irenæus, who may be said to represent the mind of S. John and of the Church, both in the East and in the West, paraphrases as follows the above passages of Scripture :—

In drawing out the parallel of the first creation and the second, of the old Adam and the new, and of the analogy between the Incarnation or natural body and the Church or mystical body of Christ, he says:[3]

---

[1] Eph. i. 19-23.   [2] S. John vii. 39.
[3] 'In fide nostra, quam perceptam ab Ecclesia custodimus, et quæ semper a Spiritu Dei, quasi in vaso bono eximium quoddam

'Our faith received from the Church, which (*receives*) always from the Spirit of God as an excellent gift in a noble vessel, always young and making young the vessel itself in which it is. For this gift of God is intrusted to the Church, as the breath of life (*was imparted*) to the first man, to this end, that all the members partaking of it might be quickened with life. And thus the communication of Christ is imparted; that is, the Holy Ghost, the earnest of incorruption, the confirmation of the faith, the way of ascent to God. For in the Church (he says) God placed apostles, prophets, doctors, and all other operations of the Spirit, of which none are partakers

depositum juvenescens, et juvenescere faciens ipsum vas in quo est. Hoc enim Ecclesiae creditum est Dei munus, quemadmodum ad inspirationem plasmationi, ad hoc ut omnia membra percipientia vivificentur; et in eo deposita est communicatio Christi. id est, Spiritus Sanctus, arrha incorruptelae, et confirmatio fidei nostrae, et scala ascensionis ad Deum. In Ecclesia enim, inquit, posuit Deus Apostolos, Prophetas, doctores, et universam reliquam operationem Spiritus: cujus non sunt participes omnes, qui non currunt ad Ecclesiam, sed semetipsos fraudant a vita, per sententiam malam, et operationem pessimam. Ubi enim Ecclesia, ibi et Spiritus Dei; et ubi Spiritus Dei, illic Ecclesia, et omnis gratia: Spiritus autem veritas. Quapropter qui non participant eum, neque a mammillis matris nutriuntur in vitam, neque percipiunt de corpore Christi procedentem nitidissimum fontem: sed effodiunt sibi lacus detritos de fossis terrenis, et de coeno putidam bibunt aquam, effugientes fidem Ecclesiae, ne traducantur; rejicientes vero Spiritum, ut non erudiantur.'—S. Iren. *Cont. Hæret.* lib. iii. cap. 24.

who do not come to the Church, thereby depriving themselves of life by a perverse mind and by worse deeds. For where the Church is, there is also the Spirit of God; and where the Spirit of God is, there is the Church and all grace. But the Spirit is truth. Wherefore they who do not partake of Him (*the Spirit*), and are not nurtured unto life at the breast of the mother (*the Church*), do not receive of that most pure fountain which proceeds from the Body of Christ, but dig out for themselves broken pools from the trenches of the earth, and drink water stained with mire, because they turn aside from the faith of the Church lest they should be convicted, and reject the Spirit lest they should be taught.'

Tertullian says, speaking of the Baptismal Creed:[1] 'But forasmuch as the attestation of (*our*) faith and the promise of our salvation are pledged by three witnesses, the mention of the Church is necessarily added, since where these are—that is, the Father, Son, and Holy Ghost—there is the Church, which is the Body of the Three.'

S. Augustine, in expounding the Creed, remarks

---

[1] 'Quum autem sub tribus et testatio fidei, et sponsio salutis pignerentur, necessario adjicitur Ecclesiæ mentio: quoniam ubi tres, id est Pater et Filius et Spiritus Sanctus, ibi Ecclesia, quæ trium corpus est.'—Tertul. *De Bapt.* sect. vi. ed. Rigalt. p. 226.

on the relation in which the article of the Church stands to the doctrine of the Holy Trinity. He says :[1] 'In like manner we ought to believe in the Holy Ghost, that the Trinity, which is God, may have its fulness. Then the Holy Church is mentioned; . . . the right order of the confession required that to the Trinity should be subjoined the Church, as the dwelling to the inhabitant, and as His temple to the Lord, and the city to its builder.'

Again he says :[2] 'For what the soul is to the body of a man, that the Holy Ghost is to the body of Christ, which is the Church. What the Holy Ghost does in the whole Church, that the soul does in all

---

[1] 'Sic credere nos et in Spiritum Sanctum, ut illa Trinitas compleatur, quæ Deus est; deinde sancta commemoratur Ecclesia. . . . Rectus itaque confessionis ordo poscebat, ut Trinitati subjungeretur Ecclesia, tamquam habitatori domus sua, et Deo templum suum, et conditori civitas sua.'—S. Aug. *Enchirid. de Fide*, cap. 56, tom. vi. p. 217.

[2] 'Quod autem est anima corpori hominis, hoc est Spiritus Sanctus corpori Christi, quod est Ecclesia: hoc agit Spiritus Sanctus in tota Ecclesia, quod agit anima in omnibus membris unius corporis. Sed videte quid caveatis, videte quid observetis, videte quid timeatis. Contingit ut in corpore humano, immo de corpore aliquod præcidatur membrum, manus, digitus, pes; numquid præcisum sequitur anima? Cum in corpore esset, vivebat; præcisum amittit vitam. Sic et homo Christianus Catholicus est, dum in corpore vivit; præcisus hæreticus factus est, membrum amputatum non sequitur Spiritus. Si ergo vultis vivere de Spiritu Sancto, tenete caritatem, amato veritatem, desiderate unitatem, ut perveniatis ad æternitatem.'— S. Aug. *Sermo in Die Pentecost. I.* tom. v. p. 1090.

the members of one body. But see what ye have to beware of, to watch over, and to fear. In the body of a man it may happen that a member, the hand, the finger, or the foot, may be cut off. Does the soul follow the severed member? While it was in the body it was alive; cut off, its life is lost. So a man is a Christian and a Catholic while he is alive in the body; cut off, he becomes a heretic. The Holy Ghost does not follow the amputated limb. If therefore ye would live by the Holy Ghost, hold fast charity, love truth, desire unity, that ye may attain unto eternity.'

And again: 'Paul the Apostle says, "One body, one spirit." Listen, members of that body. The body is made up of many members, and one spirit quickens them all. Behold, by the spirit of a man, by which I myself am a man, I hold together all the members; I command them to move; I direct the eyes to see, the ears to hear, the tongue to speak, the hands to work, the feet to walk. The offices of the members are divided severally, but one spirit holds all in one. Many are commanded, and many things are done; there is one only who commands, and one who is obeyed. What our spirit—that is, our soul—is to our members, that the Holy Ghost is to the members of Christ, to the body of Christ, which is the Church. Therefore the Apostle, when he had spoken of the one body, lest we should suppose it to be a dead body, says: "There is one body." I ask, Is this body alive? It is alive. Whence? From the one Spirit. "There is one Spirit."[1]

To this may be added a passage which has been ascribed to S. Augustine, but is probably by another hand. 'Therefore the Holy Ghost on this day (Pentecost) descended into the temple of His apostles, which He had prepared for Himself, as a shower of sanctification. (*He came*) no more as a transient visitor, but as a perpetual comforter and as an eternal inhabitant. . . . He came therefore on this day to His disciples, no longer by the grace of *visitation* and *operation*, but by the very Presence of His Majesty; and into those vessels, no longer the odour of the

---

[1] 'Paulus dicit Apostolus: *unum corpus et unus spiritus*. Membra nostra, attendite. Multis membris constitutum est corpus, et vegetat membra omnia unus spiritus. Ecce humano spiritu, quo sum ego ipse homo, membra omnia colligo: impero membris ut moveantur, intendo oculos ad videndum, aures ad audiendum, linguam ad loquendum, manus ad operandum, pedes ad ambulandum. Officia membrorum dispartita sunt, sed unus spiritus continet omnia. Multa jubentur, multa fiunt: unus jubet, uni servitur. Quod est spiritus noster, id est anima nostra, ad membra nostra; hoc Spiritus Sanctus ad membra Christi, ad corpus Christi, quod est Ecclesia. Ideo Apostolus, cùm corpus unum nominasset, ne intelligeremus mortuum corpus: *Unum* inquit *corpus*. Sed rogo te, vivit hoc corpus? Vivit. Unde? De uno spiritu.' *Et unus spiritus*.'— S. Aug. *Sermo in Die Pent. II.* tom. v. p. 1091.

balsam, but the very Substance of the sacred Unction flowed down, from whose fragrance the breadth of the whole world was to be filled, and all who came to their doctrine to be made partakers of God.'[1]

From these principles S. Augustine declares the Church to possess a mystical personality. He says: ' The Head and the body are one man, Christ and the Church are one man, a perfect man; He the bridegroom, she the bride. "And they shall be two," he says, "in one flesh."'[2]

And again he says: ' Therefore of two is made one person, of the Head and the body, of the bridegroom and the bride.' And further: 'If there are two in one flesh, *how not two in one voice?* Therefore let Christ speak, because in Christ the Church speaks, and in the Church Christ speaks, both the body in

---

[1] ' Ergo Spiritus Sanctus in hac die ad præparata sibi Apostolorum suorum templa, velut imber sanctificationis illapsus est, non jam visitator subitus, sed perpetuus consolator, et habitator æternus. . . Adfuit ergo in hac die fidelibus suis non jam per gratiam visitationis et operationis, sed per ipsam præsentiam majestatis: atque in vasa non jam odor balsami, sed ipsa substantia sacri defluxit unguenti, ex cujus fragrantia latitudo totius corporis impleretur, et appropinquantes ad eorum doctrinam, Dei fierent capaces et participes.'— S. Aug. *Sermo in Die Pent. I.* tom. v. *Append.* p. 308.

[2] ' Unus homo caput et corpus, unus homo Christus et Ecclesia, vir perfectus, ille sponsus, illa sponsa. Sed erunt, inquit, duo in carne una.'—S. Aug. *In Psalm. xviii.* tom. iv. pp. 85, 86.

the Head, and the Head in the body.'[1] 'Our Lord Jesus Christ often speaks Himself—that is, in His own Person, which is our Head—oftentimes in the person of His body, which we are, and His Church; but so that the words are heard as from the mouth of one man, that we may understand the Head and the body to consist by an integral unity, and never to be put asunder, after the manner of that matrimony of which it is said "two shall be in one flesh."'[2]

The following words of S. Gregory Nazianzen teach expressly the same doctrine: 'But now the *Holy Ghost* is given more perfectly, for He is no longer present by His *operation* as of old, but is present with us, so to speak, and converses with us in *a substantial manner*. For it was fitting that, as the Son had conversed with us in a body, the Spirit also should

---

[1] 'Fit ergo tamquam ex duobus una quædam persona, ex capite et corpore, ex sponso ex sponsa. . . . Si duo in carne una, cur non duo in voce una? Loquitur ergo Christus, quia in Christo loquitur Ecclesia, et in Ecclesia loquitur Christus; et corpus in capite, et caput in corpore.'—S. Aug. *In Psalm. xxx.* tom. iv. p. 147.

[2] 'Dominum nostrum Jesum Christum plerumque loqui ex se, id est, ex persona sua, quod est caput nostrum; plerumque ex persona corporis sui, quod sumus nos et Ecclesia ejus; sed ita quasi ex unius hominis ore sonare verba, ut intelligamus caput et corpus in unitate integritatis consistere, nec separari ab invicem: tamquam conjugium illud, de quo dictum est, Erunt duo in carne una.'—S. Aug. *In Psalm. xl.* tom. iv. p. 341.

come among us in *a bodily manner* and when Christ had returned to His own place, He should descend to us.'[1]

S. Cyril of Alexandria likewise says: 'What then is this grace? It is that pouring forth of the Spirit, as S. Paul says.' 'Therefore the Holy Ghost works in us *by Himself*, truly sanctifying us and uniting us to Himself, while He joins us to Himself and makes us partakers of the Divine nature.'[2]

---

[1] Τὸ δὲ νῦν, τελεώτερον, οὐκ ἔτι ἐνεργείᾳ παρὸν, ὡς πρότερον, οὐσιωδῶς δὲ, ὡς ἂν εἴποι τις, συγγινόμενόν τε καὶ συμπολιτευόμενον. ἔπρεπε γὰρ, Υἱοῦ σωματικῶς ἡμῖν ὁμιλήσαντος, καὶ αὐτὸ φανῆναι σωματικῶς· καὶ Χριστοῦ πρὸς ἑαυτὸν ἐπανελθόντος, ἐκεῖνο πρὸς ἡμᾶς κατελθεῖν. S. Greg. Nazian. *Orat. xli. in Pentecost.* tom. i. p. 740.

[2] Τίς οὖν ἄρα ἡ χάρις, ἢ πάντως ἡ τοῦ ἁγίου Πνεύματος χύσις ἡ ἐν ταῖς καρδίαις ἡμῶν γινομένη, κατὰ τὴν τοῦ Παύλου φωνήν ... αὐτουργὸν ἄρα τὸ Πνεῦμα ἐν ἡμῖν, ἀληθῶς ἁγιάζον καὶ ἑνοῦν ἡμᾶς ἑαυτῷ διὰ τῆς πρὸς αὐτὸ συναφείας θείας τε φύσεως ἀποτελοῦν κοινωνούς. S. Cyril. Alex. *Thesaurus de Trin. Assertio xxxiv.* tom. v. p. 352.

'Sic igitur, cum fidelibus ac justis impertiri communicarique Spiritus Sanctus legitur, non ipsamet illius persona tribui, sed ejus efficientia videri potest; idque communis fere sensus habet eorum, qui in Patrum veterum lectione minus exercitati sunt. Quos qui attente pervestigare voluerit, intelliget occultum quemdam et inusitatum missionis communicationisque modum apud illos celebrari, quo Spiritus ille divinus in justorum sese animos insinuans, cum illis copulatur; eumque non accidentarium, ut ita dicam, esse, hoc est qualitate duntaxat illa coelesti ac divina perfici. quam in pectora nostra diffundit idem coelestium donorum largitor ac procreator Spiritus, sed οὐσιώδη, hoc est substantialem, ita ut substantia ipsa Spiritus Sancti nobiscum jungatur, nosque sanctos, ac justos, ac Dei denique Filios efficiat. Ac nonnullos etiam antiquorum illorum dicentes audiet, tantum istud

S. Gregory the Great, summing up the doctrine of S. Augustine, writes as follows :—' The holy universal Church is one body, constituted under Christ Jesus its Head. . . . Therefore Christ, with His whole Church, both that which is still on earth and that which now reigns with Him in heaven, is one Person; and as the soul is one which quickens the various members of the body, so the one Holy Spirit quickens and illuminates the whole Church. For as Christ, who is the Head of the Church, was conceived of the Holy Ghost, so the Holy Church, which is His body, is filled by the same Spirit that it may have life, is confirmed by His power that it may subsist in the bond of one faith and charity. Therefore the Apostle says, "from whom the whole body being compacted and fitly joined together maketh increase of the body." This is that body out of which the Spirit quickeneth not; wherefore the blessed Augustine says, "If thou wouldst live of the Spirit of Christ, be in the Body of Christ." Of this Spirit the heretic does not live, nor the schismatic, nor the

tamque stupendum Dei beneficium tunc primum hominibus esse concessum, postquam Dei Filius homo factus ad usum hominum salutemque descendit, ut fructus iste sit adventus, ac meritorum, et sanguinis ipsius, veteris Testamenti justis hominibus nondum attributus; quibus "nondum erat Spiritus datus, quia Jesus nondum fuerat glorificatus," ut Evangelista Joannes scribit.'—Petavius, *De Trin.* lib. viii. cap. iv. p. 128.

excommunicated, for they are not of the body; but the Church hath a Spirit that giveth life, because it inheres inseparably to Christ its Head: for it is written, " He that adhereth to the Lord is one spirit with Him."' [1]

In this passage S. Gregory traces out:
1. The Head ;
2. The body ;
3. The mystical personality ;

[1] ' Unum quippe corpus est tota sancta universalis Ecclesia, sub Christo Jesu, suo videlicet capite, constituta. Unde ait Apostolus: *Ipse est caput corporis Ecclesiæ, qui est principium, primogenitus ex mortuis.* Ipsa est enim quæ per Prophetam jucundatur et dicit; *Nunc exaltavit caput meum super inimicos meos.* Pater enim Filium, qui est caput Ecclesiæ, super inimicos ejus exaltavit, cum, destructo mortis imperio, in suæ illum majestatis æqualitate constituit cui et dixit: *Sede a dextris meis, donec ponam inimicos tuos scabellum pedum tuorum.* Christus itaque cum tota sua Ecclesia, sive quæ adhuc versatur in terris, sive quæ cum eo jam regnat in cœlis, una persona est. Et sicut est una anima quæ diversa corporis membra vivificat, ita totam simul Ecclesiam unus Spiritus Sanctus vegetat et illustrat. Sicut namque Christus, qui est caput Ecclesiæ, de Spiritu Sancto conceptus est: sic sancta Ecclesia, quæ corpus ejus est, eodem Spiritu Sancto repletur ut vivat: ejus virtute firmatur, ut in unius fidei et caritatis compage subsistat. Unde dicit Apostolus: *ex quo totum corpus per nexus et conjunctiones subministratum et constructum crescit* in augmentum Dei. Istud est corpus, extra quod non vivificat spiritus. Unde dicit beatus Augustinus: *Si vis vivere de spiritu Christi, esto in corpore Christi.* De hoc spiritu non vivit hæreticus, non vivit schismaticus, non vivit excommunicatus: non enim sunt de corpore. Ecclesia autem spiritum vivificantem habet, quia capiti suo Christo inseparabiliter adhaeret. Scriptum est enim: *Qui adhaeret Domino unus spiritus est cum eo.*'
—S. Greg. *Expos. in Psal. v. Pænit.* tom. iii. p. 511.

4. The conception;

5. The intrinsic and extrinsic unity of the Church, and the grace of sanctity and life, which is given by the Church alone.

Hitherto I have refrained from doing more than trace out the meaning of the passages of Scripture and of the Fathers above cited. I will now go on to draw certain conclusions from them.

And, first, it is evident that the present dispensation, under which we are, is the dispensation of the Spirit, or of the Third Person of the Holy Trinity. To Him in the Divine economy, has been committed the office of applying the redemption of the Son to the souls of men, by the vocation, justification, and salvation of the elect. We are, therefore, under the personal guidance of the Third Person as truly as the Apostles were under the guidance of the Second. The presence of the Eternal Son, by incarnation, was the centre of their unity: the presence of the Eternal Spirit, by the incorporation of the mystical body, is the centre of unity to us.

Again, it is evident that this dispensation of the Spirit, since the incarnation of the Son, and from the day of Pentecost, differs in many critical and characteristic ways from His presence and office in the world before the advent of Jesus Christ. It differs not only in exuberance of gifts and graces, nor only in its miraculous manifestations, nor again in its universality, as if what was given before in measure was given afterwards in fulness, but in a deeper way, that is, in the office which He has assumed, and in the manner of His presence.

I. And, first, the Holy Ghost came before into the world by His universal operations in all mankind, but now He comes through the Incarnate Son by a special and personal presence.

As the Son of God has both an eternal generation and a temporal mission,—that is, His eternal generation from the Father,[1] and His temporal advent by incarnation,—so the Spirit of God has likewise an eternal procession and a temporal mission from the Father and the Son. The eternal mission is the Passive Spiration, whereby the Person and relations of the Holy Ghost to the Father and to the Son are eternally constituted. And this by the Fathers and Theologians[2] is called His eternal procession. The temporal mission of the Holy Ghost began from the day of Pentecost, when He came to us through the Incarnate Son. S. Augustine teaches that this was signified by the material breath with which Jesus

---

[1] Petav. *De Trinitate,* lib. viii. cap. 2.
[2] Petav. *De Trinitate,* lib. vii. cap. 18, sec. 5, 6.

breathed upon His Apostles, when He said, 'Receive ye the Holy Ghost.'[1] It was the symbol and pledge of the gift which He had promised to them. It was reserved till He should be glorified. Then, on His Ascension to the right hand of God, the Holy Ghost was sent from the Father and the Son incarnate. S. Augustine calls the day of Pentecost the Dies Natalis or Nativity of the Holy Ghost. The Spirit of God had wrought before throughout the whole race descended from the first Adam. He came now by a special and personal mission to work in the children of the second Adam. The first Adam by sin forfeited for himself and for us the presence and grace of the Holy Ghost; the second Adam has restored to His children the presence and the grace which had been lost; but with this difference—the first Adam was man, the second Adam is God. The first, though sinless, was capable of sinning; the second, being God, could not sin. The Holy Ghost proceeds from the second Adam to us who are born again in the new creation of God.

What has here been stated is expressed by S. Thomas [2] as follows:—On the question whether

---

[1] S. August. *De Gen. ad Lit.* tom. iii. p. 260. *De Trin.* lib. iv. tom. viii. p. 829.

[2] 'Respondeo dicendum quod in his quæ important originem

mission be eternal or temporal only, he says, 'It is to be said that in those things which imply the

divinarum personarum, est quædam differentia attendenda. Quædam enim in sua significatione important solum habitudinem ad principium, ut *processio* et *exitus*. Quædam vero cum habitudine ad principium determinant processionis terminum. Quorum quædam determinant terminum æternum sicut *generatio* et *spiratio*; nam generatio est processio divinæ personæ in naturam divinam, et spiratio passive accepta importat processionem amoris subsistentis. Quædam vero cum habitudine ad principium important terminum temporalem, sicut *missio* et *datio*. Mittitur enim aliquid ad hoc ut sit in aliquo, et datur ad hoc quod habeatur. Personam autem divinam haberi ab aliqua creatura, vel esse novo modo existendi in ea, est quoddam temporale.—Unde *missio* et *datio* in divinis dicuntur temporaliter tantum; *generatio* autem et *spiratio* solum ab æterno; *processio* autem et *exitus* dicuntur in divinis et æternaliter, et temporaliter; nam Filius ab æterno processit, ut sit Deus; temporaliter autem, ut etiam sit homo secundum missionem visibilem, vel etiam ut sit in homine secundum invisibilem missionem.

'Facta autem est missio visibilis ad Christum in baptismo quidem sub specie columbæ, quod est animal fecundum, ad ostendendum in Christo auctoritatem donandi gratiam per spiritualem regenerationem; . . . . In transfiguratione vero sub specie nubis lucidæ, ad ostendendum exuberantiam doctrinæ; . . . . Ad apostolos autem sub specie flatus, ad ostendendam potestatem ministerii in dispensatione sacramentorum; unde dictum est eis, *Quorum remiseritis peccata, remittuntur eis.* Sed sub linguis ignois, ad ostendendum officium doctrinæ: unde dicitur, quod *cœperunt loqui variis linguis.* Ad patres autem veteris Testamenti missio visibilis Spiritus Sancti fieri non debuit; quia prius debuit perfici missio visibilis Filii quam Spiritus Sancti, cum Spiritus Sanctus manifestet Filium, sicut Filius Patrem. Fuerunt autem factæ visibiles apparitiones divinarum personarum patribus veteris Testamenti; quæ quidem missiones visibiles dici non possunt, quia non fuerunt factæ (secundum Augustinum, lib. 2, de Trin. cap. 17, circa fin.) ad designandum inhabitationem divinæ personæ per gratiam, sed ad

origin of Divine Persons a distinction is to be observed. For some things, by their signification, imply only the relation to their principle, as procession and going forth; and some, together with the relation to their principle, determine the end for which they proceed. Of these some determine the eternal end, as generation and spiration; for generation is the procession of a Divine Person in the Divine Nature, and spiration, taken passively, implies the procession of love subsisting (in the nature of God). Other things with the relation to their principle imply the temporal end, as mission and gift; for a thing is sent for this end that it may exist in another, and given to this end that it may be possessed. But that a Divine Person should be possessed by any creature, or should be in it by a new mode of existence, is something temporal. Therefore mission and gift in things divine are predicated in a temporal sense alone; but generation and spiration are predicated only of eternity. But procession and going forth are predicated in things divine both eternally and temporally. From eternity He proceeds as God, but temporally as Man also by a visible mission; and also that He may be in man by a mission

aliquid aliud manifestandum.'—S. Thomæ *Sum. Theol.* prima pars, quæst. xliii. art. 2, 7.

which is invisible.'[1] And further, he adds, speaking of the mission of the Holy Ghost, ' But the visible mission was fulfilled to Christ in His baptism under the form of a dove—which is a fruitful creature—to manifest the authority of bestowing grace by spiritual regeneration which was in Christ. . . . But in the transfiguration, under the form of a shining cloud, to manifest the exuberance of His teaching. . . . But to the Apostles, under the form of breath, to manifest the power of the ministry in the dispensation of sacraments; wherefore He said to them, "Whosesoever sins you forgive they are forgiven unto them." But in tongues of fire to manifest the office of teaching, wherefore it is written, "They began to speak with various tongues." But to the Fathers of the Old Testament it was not fitting that the mission of the Holy Ghost should be visibly fulfilled, because it was fitting that the visible mission of the Son should first be fulfilled before that of the Holy Ghost, forasmuch as the Holy Ghost manifests the Son, as the Son manifests the Father. But visible apparitions of Divine Persons were made to the Fathers of the Old Testament, which, however, cannot be called visible missions, because they were not made, as S. Augus-

---

[1] Divi Thomæ *Sum. Theol.* prima pars, quæst. xliii. artic. 2.

tine says, to designate the inhabitation of a Divine Person by grace, but to manifest something else.'

After profusely expounding these articles of S. Thomas, Suarez adds the following words, which are very much to our purpose: 'And here a distinction may be noted between the mission of the Word . . . and this mission of the Spirit; . . . that the mission of the Word is without merit given by the charity of God alone, according to the words of S. John,—" God so loved the world, that He gave His only-begotten Son;" but the mission of the Holy Ghost is given through the merits of the Word, and therefore the Spirit was not given until Jesus was glorified. Which Christ Himself also declared, saying, " I will pray the Father, and He shall give you another Paraclete." '[1]

II. The second characteristic difference is, that the Holy Ghost came to create the mystical body of Christ.

Until the day of Pentecost the mystical body was

---

[1] Unde notari potest discrimen inter missionem Verbi, et hanc missionem Spiritus (idemque fere est de aliis), quod missio Verbi absque merito sola Dei charitate facta est, juxta illud Joann. 3: *Sic Deus dilexit mundum, ut Filium suum unigenitum daret*: missio autem Spiritus Sancti ex merito Verbi facta est: ideo enim non fuit Spiritus datus, donec Jesus fuit glorificatus. Quod etiam significavit ipse Christus dicens: *Ego rogabo Patrem, et alium Paracletum dabit vobis.*—Suarez, *in prim. part. S. Thom.* lib. xii. cap. 6, sect. 26.

not complete. There could be no body till there was a Head. There was no Head until the Son was incarnate; and, even when incarnate, the completion of the body was deferred until the Head was glorified; that is, until the Incarnate Son had fulfilled His whole redeeming office in life, death, resurrection, and ascension, returning to enthrone the Humanity with which His eternal Person was invested, at the right hand of the Father. Then, when the Head was exalted in His supreme majesty over angels and men, the creation and organisation of the body was completed.

All that had gone before was but type and shadow. The people of Israel, organised and bound together by their Priesthood, and by the ceremonies and ritual of the Tabernacle and the Temple, had but 'a shadow of things to come, but the body is Christ's.'[1] It was a Church after the measures and proportions of the times which then were. But it had no Incarnate Head, no Divine Person proceeding from that Head to inhabit and to guide it. Its sacraments were shadows, working *ex opere operantis*, by the faith of the receiver, not by the divine virtue which went out from them. Its sacrifices and priesthood were real in relation to the order which then was, but

[1] Col. ii. 17.

only shadows of the sacrifice and priesthood of the Incarnate Son, and of His Church which is now.[1]

What has here been affirmed may be proved by the following propositions:—

(1.) That Christ, as Head of the Church, is the fountain of all sanctity to His mystical body. 'In Him it hath well-pleased the Father that all fulness should dwell.'[2] 'He hath made Him Head over all the Church, which is His body, and the fulness of Him who is filled all in all.'[3] S. Gregory the Great says: 'For the Mediator between God and men, the man Christ Jesus, has present always and in all things Him who also proceeds from Himself by substance, namely, the same Spirit. In the saints who declare Him He abides, but in the Mediator He abides in fulness. Because in them He abides by grace for a special purpose, but in Him He abides by substance and for all things.'[4] S. Augustine says: 'Is there

---

[1] I am aware that Tournelly appears to be contrary to this statement; but not only the stream of theologians is against him, but his argument, though perhaps not his words, may be shown to agree in substance with what is stated in the text.—*De Ecclesia*, quæst. i. art. 3.

[2] Col. i. 19. [3] Eph. i. 22, 23.

[4] 'Mediator autem Dei et hominum, homo Christus Jesus, in cunctis eum et semper et continuè habet præsentem: quia et ex illo idem Spiritus per substantiam profertur. Rectè ergo et cum in sanctis prædicatoribus maneat, in Mediatore singulariter manere perhibetur: quia in istis per gratiam manet ad aliquid, in illo autem per sub-

then any other difference between that Head and the excellence of any member beside, that all the fulness of the Divinity dwells in that body as in a temple? Plainly there is. Because, by a special assumption of that Humanity, one Person with the Word is constituted. That assumption then was singular, and has nothing common with any men by whatsoever wisdom and holiness they may be sanctified.'[1] And again he says: 'It is one thing to be made wise by the wisdom of God, and another to bear the Personality of God's wisdom. For though the nature of the body of the Church be the same, who does not understand that there is a great distance between the Head and the members?'[2]

(2.) That the sanctification of the Church is ef-

stantiam manet ad cuncta.'—S. Greg. *Moral.* lib. ii. cap. ult. tom. i. p. 73.

[1] 'An etiam præter hoc, quod tamquam in templo in illo corpore habitat omnis plenitudo divinitatis, est aliud quod intersit inter illud caput et cujuslibet membri excellentiam? Est plane, quod singulari quadam susceptione hominis illius una facta est persona cum Verbo. . . . Singularis est ergo illa susceptio, nec cum hominibus aliquibus sanctis, quantalibet sapientia et sanctitate præstantibus, ullo modo potest esse communis.'—S. Aug. Ep. clxxxvii. 40, tom. ii. p. 691.

[2] 'Aliud est enim sapientem tantùm fieri per Sapientiam Dei, et aliud ipsam Personam sustinere Sapientiæ Dei. Quamvis enim eadem natura sit corporis Ecclesiæ, multum distare inter caput et membra cetera quis non intelligat?'—S. Aug. *De Agone Christiano*, cap. 22, tom. vi. p. 254.

fected by the gift of the Holy Ghost. Forasmuch as it is 'built together into an habitation of God in the Spirit;'[1] 'and the charity of God is poured out in our hearts by the Holy Ghost who is given unto us.'[2]

This proposition needs no further proof than the fact, that the Church is gathered from the world by baptism, and that into every soul rightly baptized the graces of Faith, Hope, and Charity are infused, together with the seven gifts, and a substantial union of the Holy Ghost with the soul is constituted. The sanctification therefore of souls is effected, not only by the effusion of created graces, but also by the personal indwelling of the Sanctifier, and by their union with the uncreated sanctity of the Spirit of God. 'Know you not that you are the temple of God, and that the Spirit of God dwelleth in you? .. For the temple of God is holy, which (*temple*) you are.'[3] S. Athanasius says: 'We abide in God, and He in us, because He hath given us of His Spirit. But if by the presence of the Spirit who is in us we are made partakers of the Divine Nature, he is beside himself who shall say that this is done by a creature, and not by the Spirit of God. For the same cause He is in men, and they in whom He is are deified. But He

---

[1] Eph. ii, 22.   [2] Rom. v. 5.
[3] 1 Cor. iii. 16, 17.

who deifies, beyond all doubt, His nature is the nature of God.'[1] Again, S. Cyril says : 'Christ is formed in us by the Holy Ghost imparting to us a kind of Divine form by sanctification and justification.'[2]

(3.) That the Holy Ghost dwells personally and substantially in the mystical body, which is the incorporation of those who are sanctified. This follows from the last and needs no further proof.

(4.) That the members of the mystical body who are sanctified, partake not only of the created graces, but of a substantial union with the Holy Ghost. This has been already proved above.

(5.) That this substantial union of the Holy Ghost with the mystical body, though analogous to the hypostatic union, is not hypostatic ; forasmuch as the human personality of the members of Christ still subsists in this substantial union. [3]

I forbear to add more to this second distinction; but I would refer those who desire to see it fully

---

[1] Εἰ δὲ τῇ τοῦ Πνεύματος μετουσίᾳ γινόμεθα κοινωνοὶ θείας φύσεως· μαίνοιτ' ἂν τις λέγων τὸ Πνεῦμα τῆς κτιστῆς φύσεως, καὶ μὴ τῆς τοῦ Θεοῦ. διὰ τοῦτο γὰρ καὶ ἐν οἷς γίνεται, οὗτοι θεοποιοῦνται· εἰ δὲ θεοποιεῖ, οὐκ ἀμφίβολον ὅτι ἡ τούτου φύσις Θεοῦ ἐστι. S. Athan. *Ep. I. ad Serapionem*, cap. 24, tom. ii. p. 672.

[2] Μορφοῦταί γε μὴν ἐν ἡμῖν ὁ Χριστὸς, ἐνιέντος ἡμῖν τοῦ ἁγίου πνεύματος θείαν τινὰ μόρφωσιν, δι' ἁγιασμοῦ καὶ δικαιοσύνης. S. Cyril. Alex. *In Isaiam*, lib. iv. orat. 2, tom. ii. p. 591.

[3] Petav. *De Trinitate*, lib. viii. cap. 7, § 12.

treated, to the tenth chapter of the Sixth Book, *De Incarnatione Verbi*, in the *Theologia Dogmatica* of Thomassinus. We may therefore proceed to another distinction.

III. Thirdly, a further characteristic difference is constituted by the indissoluble union between the Holy Ghost and the mystical body. Before the Incarnation, the Holy Spirit wrought in the souls of men one by one, illuminating, converting, sanctifying, and perfecting the elect. But the union between His presence and the soul was conditional on the correspondence and fidelity of the individual. It was a dissoluble union, and in the multitudes who fell from grace it was actually dissolved. In the faithful, as in Enoch and in Daniel, that union was sustained to the end. In the unfaithful, as in Saul and in Solomon, after their great graces, it was dissolved. We also are under the same law of individual probation. If we persevere in faith, hope, charity, and contrition, the union between us and the presence of the Holy Spirit in us remains firm. If we fail, we dissolve it. It is therefore conditional, depending upon our finite, frail, and unstable will. And yet such is the strange and superficial view of those who have been deprived of the perfect light of faith by the great spiritual anarchy of the last three hundred years. Having lost the conception of the Church as distinct from a multitude of individuals told by number, they suppose the union of the Holy Spirit with the Church to be also conditional and dissoluble.

It is manifest, however, that the union of the Holy Ghost with the Church is not conditional, but absolute, depending upon no finite will, but upon the Divine will alone, and therefore indissoluble to all eternity. For it is constituted (1) by the union of the Holy Ghost with the Head of the Church, not only as God but as Man, and in both these relations this union is indissoluble. It is constituted further (2) by His union with the mystical body, which, as a body, is imperishable, though individuals in it may perish. There will never come a time when that body will cease to be, and therefore there will never come a time when the Holy Ghost will cease to be united to it. The mystical body will exist to all eternity in the perfect number of the blessed. These Divine unions, namely, first, of the Head with the members; next, of the members with each other; and, lastly, of the Holy Ghost with the body, will be likewise eternal. And in the state of glory the perfect personal identity and perfect mutual recognition of the saints in all their orders will perpetuate that which here constitutes the symmetry and perfection of the Church

But that which shall be eternal is indissoluble also in time—the union, that is, of the Spirit with the body as a whole. Individuals may fall from it as multitudes have fallen; provinces, nations, particular churches may fall from it; but the body still remains, its unity undivided, its life indefectible. And that because the line of the faithful is never broken; the chain of the elect is always woven link within link, and wound together in the mysterious course and onward movement of truth and grace in the hearts and wills of the regenerate. The line of faith, hope, and charity is never dissolved. The threefold cord cannot be broken, and the ever-blessed Trinity always inhabits His tabernacle upon earth—the souls of the elect, who 'are builded together into an habitation of God in the Spirit.'[1] The union therefore of the Spirit with the body can never be dissolved. It is a Divine act, analogous to the hypostatic union, whereby the two natures of God and man are eternally united in one Person. So the mystical body, the head and the members, constitute one mystical person; and the Holy Ghost inhabiting that body, and diffusing His created grace throughout it, animates it as the soul quickens the body of a man.

From this flow many truths. First, the Church is

[1] Eph. ii. 22.

not an individual, but a mystical person, and all its endowments are derived from the Divine Person of its Head, and the Divine Person who is its Life. As in the Incarnation there is a communication of the Divine perfections to the humanity, so in the Church the perfections of the Holy Spirit become the endowments of the body. It is imperishable, because He is God; indivisibly one, because He is numerically one; holy, because He is the fountain of holiness; infallible both in believing and in teaching, because His illumination and His voice are immutable, and therefore, being not an individual depending upon the fidelity of a human will, but a body depending only on the Divine will, it is not on trial or probation, but is itself the instrument of probation to mankind. It cannot be affected by the frailty or sins of the human will, any more than the brightness of the firmament by the dimness or the loss of human sight. It can no more be tainted by human sin than the holy sacraments, which are always immutably pure and divine, though all who come to them be impure and faithless. What the Church was in the beginning it is now, and ever shall be in all the plenitude of its divine endowments, because the union between the body and the Spirit is indissoluble, and all the operations of the Spirit in the body are perpetual and absolute.

The multitude and fellowship of the just who, from Abel to the Incarnation, had lived and died in faith and union with God, constituted the soul of a body which should be hereafter. They did not constitute the body, but they were waiting for it. They did not constitute the Church, which signifies not only the *election* but the *aggregation* of the servants of God; not only the calling out, but the calling together into one all those who are united to Him. Some of the Fathers do indeed speak of them as the Church, because they were to the then world what the Church is now to the world of to-day. They belong also to the Church, though it did not then exist, just as the Lamb was slain from the foundation of the world, though the sacrifice on Calvary was four thousand years deferred. All grace was from the beginning given through the Most Precious Blood, though as yet it had not been shed. So the mystical body had its members, though as yet it was not created. They were admitted to it when the kingdom of heaven was opened to them and the Incarnate Word was exalted to His glory as Head over all things to the Church.

As then till the Incarnation there was no Incarnate Head, so till the day of Pentecost there was no complete organisation. The members were not united to the Head, nor to each other, nor as a body to the Holy Ghost. But it is these three Divine unions which constitute the organisation of the mystical body. And these three unions were constituted by the mission of the Holy Ghost from the Incarnate Son, and by His descent and inhabitation in the members of Christ.

IV. The fourth difference is that whereas the Holy Ghost wrought invisibly before the Incarnation, He has by His temporal mission manifested His presence and His operations by the Visible Church of Jesus Christ.

1. The Church is the evidence of His presence among men. Before the Incarnation He wrought unseen, and by no revealed law of His operations. Now He has assumed the mystical body as the *visible incorporation* of His presence, and the revealed channel of His grace. The Visible Church is a creation so purely divine, and its endowments are so visibly supernatural, that it can be referred to no cause or origin below God.

(1) The Church witnesses to the presence of a Divine Person by its supernatural unity. The first formation of its unity by the assimilation of the intellects and wills of men who had never agreed before, and of nations, races, and kingdoms perpetually anta-

gonist, and perpetually contending about everything but the faith, is a work self-evidently divine.

The wonderful world-wide coherence of this unity, resisting all the solvents of human subtlety and all the efforts of human strength, and perpetuating itself through all antagonisms and through all ages undivided and indivisible, is evidence of a power higher than man. S. Augustine asks: 'What did the advent of the Holy Ghost accomplish? How did He teach us his presence? How did He manifest it? They all spoke with the tongues of all nations. . . . One man spoke with the tongues of all nations. The unity of the Church is in the tongues of all nations. Behold here the unity of the Catholic Church diffused throughout the world is declared.'[1] Again: 'Wherefore as then (Pentecost) the tongues of all nations showed the presence of the Holy Ghost in one man, so now the charity of the unity of all nations shows Him to be here.'[2]

---

[1] 'Quid ipse adventus Spiritus Sancti, quid egit? Præsentiam suam unde docuit? unde monstravit? Linguis omnium gentium locuti sunt omnes. . . . Loquebatur unus homo linguis omnium gentium: unitas Ecclesiæ in linguis omnium gentium. Ecce et hic unitas Ecclesiæ catholicæ commendatur toto orbe diffusæ.'—S. Aug. *Sermo in Die Pent. ii.* tom. v. p. 1091.

[2] 'Quamobrem sicut tunc indicabant adesse Spiritum Sanctum in uno homine linguæ omnium gentium: sic cum nunc caritas indicat unitatis omnium gentium.'—S. Aug. *Sermo in Die Pent. iii.* tom. v. p. 1094.

(2) Secondly, it witnesses for a supernatural presence by its imperishableness in the midst of all the works of man, which are perpetually resolving themselves again into the dust out of which they were taken.

(3) Thirdly, the Visible Church witnesses to the presence of the Spirit of Truth by its immutability in doctrine of faith, and morals.

And all these truths point to the presence of a Divine Power and Person, by whom alone such gifts could be communicated to men. The visible incorporation of the Church therefore becomes the manifestation of His presence. 'One body, one Spirit,' is not only a fact, but a revelation. We know that there is the Spirit because there is the body. The body is one because the Spirit is one. The unity of the Holy Ghost is the intrinsic reason of the unity of the Church. Because His illumination is one and changeless, its intelligence is one and immutable. Because His charity never varies, therefore the unity of its communion can never be suspended. He organises and unfolds the mystical body, His own presence being the centre of its unity and the principal of its cohesion. What the dove was at Jordan, and the tongues of fire at Pentecost, that the one visible Church is now; the witness of the mission, advent, and perpetual presence of the Spirit of the Father and of the Son.

2. It is, further, the instrument of His power.

And that, first, by the perpetuity and diffusion of the light of the Incarnation throughout the world and throughout all time.

Next, by the perpetuity of sanctifying grace. And that by the perpetuity of the Seven Sacraments, which initiate and envelope the whole spiritual life of man from birth to death, sanctifying the soul in all its ages, and relations to God and to human life, and organising the Church perpetually, multiplying its members by baptism, renewing the body as it is diminished by natural death, propagating by the spiritual generation the line of its pastors, and giving to it a supernatural centre and solidity in the sacrament of the altar, which in the midst of the other sacraments, that are transient, abides for ever, the permanent presence of the Word made flesh in the tabernacle of God with men.

3. Thirdly, in virtue of the perpetual presence of the Holy Ghost united indissolubly to the body of Christ, not only the ordinary and sacramental actions of grace are perpetual, but also the extraordinary operations and gifts of miracles, visions, and prophecy abide always in the Church, not in all men,

nor manifested at all times, but present always, distributed to His servants severally at His will, and for the ends known to His wisdom, sometimes revealed, sometimes hidden from us.

4. Lastly, the body of Christ is the organ of His voice.

Our Lord has said, 'He that heareth you heareth me.' 'Ye shall be witnesses unto me.' 'Go ye into all the world and preach the Gospel to every creature.' 'He that despiseth, despiseth not man, but God.'[1] How should these things be true, or rather how should not these words be most illusory and false, if the perpetual, living voice of the Church in all ages were not identified with the voice of Jesus Christ? S. Augustine asks, as we have already seen, with the point and power which is his own,—If the body and the head, Christ and the Church, be one flesh, how are they not also one voice?' 'Si in carne unâ, quomodo non in voce unâ?'

To sum up, then, what has been said in the language of theology.

1. First, from the indissoluble union of the Holy Spirit with the Church flow the three *properties* of Unity, Visibleness, and Perpetuity.

Unity is the intrinsic unity of intelligence, will,

[1] 1 Thess. iv. 8.

and organisation, generated from within by the unity of the Person and the operation of the Holy Ghost. The property of Unity is not extrinsic and constitutional, but intrinsic and essential.

Next, the property of Visibleness is a necessary consequence of the constitution of a body or a society of men bound by public laws of worship and practice.

Lastly, Perpetuity is a necessary consequence of the indissoluble union of the soul with the body, of the Spirit with the Church.

2. From the same indissoluble union flow next the *endowments* of the Church; namely, Indefectibility in life and duration, Infallibility in teaching, and Authority in governing the flock of Jesus Christ.

These are effects springing from the same substantial union of the Holy Spirit with the Church, and reside by an intrinsic necessity in the mystical body.

3. Lastly, the four *Notes*: Unity, which is the external manifestation of the intrinsic and divine unity of which we have spoken. Unity, as a property, is the source and cause of unity as a note. Next, Sanctity, which also flows by a necessity from the union of the Holy Ghost, the Sanctifier, with the mystical body, to which a twofold sanctity is im-

parted: namely, the created grace of sanctity which resides in all the just; and the substantial union of the just with the uncreated sanctity of the Holy Ghost. Thirdly, Catholicity, or universality, that is, not mere extension, but also identity in all places; and, lastly, Apostolicity, or conformity with its original—the mission and institution of the Apostles.

These four notes strike the eye of the world, because they lie upon the surface. But the endowments and the properties are the ultimate motives into which the faithful resolve their submission to the Church of God. They believe, through the Church, in Him who is the fountain of all its supernatural gifts, God the Holy Ghost always present, the perpetual and Divine Teacher of the revelation of God, 'the Truth as it is in Jesus.'

V. The fifth and last distinction I will note between the presence and manner of operation of the Holy Ghost before the Incarnation and His own Temporal Mission in the world is this: whereas, before that epoch of the Divine Economy, the Holy Spirit taught and sanctified individuals, and spoke by the Prophets by virtue of His light and power, but with an intermittent exercise of His visitations, now He is present personally and substantially in the body of Christ, and both teaches and sanctifies, without intermission, with a perpetual divine voice and a perpetual sanctifying power; or, in other words, the divine action of the day of Pentecost is permanent, and pervades the world as far as the Church is diffused, and pervades all ages, the present as fully as the past, to-day as fully as in the beginning; or, again in other words, both theological and conventional, the living Church in every age is the sole divine channel of the revelation of God, and the infallible witness and teacher of the truths therein revealed.

Before I enter further into the exposition and proof of this proposition, I will at once point out its bearing upon what is called the rule of Faith, *i.e.* the test whereby to know what we are to believe. In the last analysis there can be conceived only three such rules; namely—

1. First, the voice of a living judge and teacher, both of doctrines and of their interpretation, guided by the assistance of the same Person who gave the original revelation, and inspired the writers of Holy Scripture, or, in other words, the same Holy Spirit from whom in the beginning both the Faith and the Scriptures were derived, perpetually preserving the same, and declaring them through the Church as His organ:

2. Secondly, the Scripture, interpreted by the

reason of individuals in dependence on their natural and supernatural light: or,

3. Thirdly, Scripture and antiquity, interpreted both by individuals, and by local or particular Churches appealing to the faith of the first centuries and to the councils held before the division of the East and West.

Now, it will be observed, that these three propositions resolve themselves into two only. They do not so much enunciate three rules, as two judges proceeding by two distinct processes. The first is the living Church proceeding by the perpetual presence and assistance of the Spirit of God in the custody and declaration of the original revelation.

The two last are resolvable into one; that is, the individual reason proceeding either by Scripture alone, or by Scripture and antiquity. But these are identical processes. The matter differs in its nature and extent, the process is one and the same.

There can be ultimately no intermediate between the Divine mind declaring itself through an organ of its own creation, or the human mind judging for itself upon the evidence and contents of revelation. There is or there is not a perpetual Divine Teacher in the midst of us. The human reason must be either the disciple or the critic of revelation.

Now, I shall dismiss at once the rule which constitutes the individual as the judge of Scripture, or of Scripture and antiquity. It is already rejected even by many Protestants. They who hold it in either form are of two classes: either pious persons, who make a conscience of not reasoning about the grounds of their faith, or such as are still—as many were once—simply entangled in a circle which is never discovered until the divine fact of the presence and office of the Holy Ghost in the mystical body becomes intelligible to them.

The only form of the question I will now notice is as follows:—There are some who appeal from the voice of the living Church to antiquity; professing to believe that while the Church was united it was infallible; that when it became divided it ceased to speak infallibly; and that the only certain rule of faith is to believe that which the Church held and taught while yet it was united and therefore infallible. Such reasoners fail to observe, that since the supposed division, and cessation of the infallible voice, there remains no divine certainty as to what was then infallibly taught. To affirm that this or that doctrine was taught then where it is now disputed, is to beg the question. The infallible Church of the first six centuries— that is, before the division—was infallible to those who lived in those ages, but is not infallible to us. It spoke to them; to us it is silent. Its infallibility does not reach to us, for the Church of the last twelve hundred years is by the hypothesis fallible, and may therefore err in delivering to us what was taught before the division. And it is certain that either the East or the West, as it is called, must err in this, for they contradict each other as to the faith before the division. I do not speak of the protests of later separations, because no one can invest them with an infallibility which they not only disclaim for themselves, but deny anywhere to exist.

Now, this theory of an infallible undivided Church then and a Church divided and fallible now proceeds on two assumptions, or rather contains in itself two primary errors. It denies the indivisible unity of the Church, and the perpetual voice of the Holy Ghost. And both these errors are resolvable into one and the same master error, the denial of the true and indissoluble union between the Holy Ghost and the Church of Jesus Christ. From this one error all errors of these later ages flow.

The indissoluble union of the Holy Ghost with the Church carries these two truths as immediate consequences: first, that the unity of the Church is absolute, numerical, and indivisible, like the unity of nature in God, and of the personality in Jesus Christ: and secondly, that its infallibility is perpetual.

(1.) S. Cyprian says, 'Unus Deus, unus Christus, una Ecclesia.' And this extrinsic unity springs from the intrinsic—that is, from the presence and operations of the Holy Ghost, by whom the body is inhabited, animated, and organised. One principle of life cannot animate two bodies, or energise in two organisations. One mind and one will fuses and holds in perfect unity the whole multitude of the faithful throughout all ages, and throughout all the world. The unity of faith, hope, and charity—the unity of the one common Teacher—renders impossible all discrepancies of belief and of worship, and renders unity of communion, not a constitutional law or an external rule of discipline, but an intrinsic necessity and an inseparable property and expression of the internal and supernatural unity of the mystical body under one Head and animated by one Spirit. It is manifest, therefore, that division is impossible. The unity of the Church refuses to be numbered in plurality. To talk of Roman, Greek, and Anglican Churches, is to deny the Articles, 'I believe in the Holy Ghost, the Holy Catholic Church,' and the Divine relation constituted between them. The relation is a Divine fact, and its enunciation is a Divine truth. S. Bede says, with a wonderful precision and depth, 'If every kingdom divided against itself is brought to desolation, for that reason the kingdom of the Father, Son, and Holy Ghost is not divided.'[1]

(2.) And next, as the unity is perpetual, so is the infallibility. Once infallible, always infallible: in the first, in the fifth, in the fifteenth, in the nineteenth century: the Divine Teacher always present, and the organ of His voice always the same. A truncated infallibility is impossible. To affirm that it has been suspended because of the sins of men, denies the perpetuity of the office of the Holy Ghost, and even of His presence; for to suppose Him present but dormant, is open to the reproach of Elias; to suppose His office to be suspended, is to conceive of the Divine Teacher after the manner of men. And further: this theory denies altogether the true and divine character of the mystical body as a creation of God, distinct from all individuals, and superior to them all: not on probation, because not dependent on any human will, but on the Divine will alone; and, therefore, not subject to

---

[1] 'Si autem omne regnum in scipsum divisum desolatur; ergo Patris et Filii et Spiritus Sancti regnum non est divisum.'—*Hom. Ven. Bed. in cap. xi. S. Luc.*

human infirmity, but impeccable, and the instrument of probation to the world. All these truths are denied in a mass by the assertion that the Church has been divided, and has, therefore, been unable to teach, as it did before, with an infallible voice. And not these truths only are denied, but many more, on which the true constitution and endowments of the Church depend.

We will now return to the fifth difference of which I began to speak, namely, the perpetual plenitude of the office and operations of the Holy Ghost in all ages, in and through the Church, both as the Author of all grace by ordinary and extraordinary supernatural operations, and as the Witness, Judge, and Teacher of all truth in and by the Church, the organ of His perpetual voice to mankind.

It is, I believe, admitted by all that the sacramental and sanctifying graces of the Holy Spirit continue to this day as they were in the beginning; or, in other words, that the office of the Holy Ghost as the Sanctifier is perpetual in all its fulness.

How is it that anyone can fail to perceive that the condition of our sanctification is Truth, and that the perpetuity of the office of the Sanctifier presupposes the perpetuity of the office of the Illuminator? These two prerogatives of the Holy Ghost are coordinate, and I may say commensurate—that is, both continue to this day in all fulness as at the first.

Now, the office of the Holy Spirit as the Illuminator has a special promise of perpetuity. It is under the character of this Spirit of Truth that our Lord promises that He should 'abide with us for ever.'[1] 'He shall bring all things to your mind,'[2] not to the Apostles only, but to all 'who should believe in their word.'

And this office of the Holy Ghost consists in the following operations: First, in the original illumination and revelation in the minds of the Apostles, and through them to the Church throughout the world.

Secondly, in the preservation of that which was revealed, or, in other words, in the prolongation of the light of truth by which the Church in the beginning was illuminated. The Light of the Church never wanes, but is permanent. 'The city has no need of the sun, nor of the moon, to shine in it. For the glory of God doth enlighten it; and the Lamb is the lamp thereof.'[3]

Thirdly, in assisting the Church to conceive, with greater fulness, explicitness, and clearness, the original truth in all its relations.

Fourthly, in defining that truth in words, and in

[1] S. John xiv. 16.   [2] S. John xiv. 26.   [3] Apoc. xxi. 23.

the creation of a sacred terminology, which becomes a permanent tradition and a perpetual expression of the original revelation.

Lastly, in the perpetual enunciation and proposition of the same immutable truth in every age. The Holy Spirit, through the Church, enunciates to this day the original revelation with an articulate voice, which never varies or falters. Its voice to-day is identical with the voice of every age, and is therefore identical with the voice of Jesus Christ. 'He that heareth you heareth Me.' It is the voice of Jesus Christ Himself, for the Holy Ghost 'receives' of the Son that which 'He shews to us.'[1]

And this office of enunciating and proposing the faith is accomplished through the human lips of the pastors of the Church. The pastoral authority, or the Episcopate, together with the priesthood and the other orders, constitute an organised body, divinely ordained to guard the deposit of the Faith. The voice of that body, not as so many individuals, but as a body, is the voice of the Holy Ghost. The pastoral ministry as a body cannot err, because the Holy Spirit, who is indissolubly united to the mystical body, is eminently and above all united to the hierarchy and body of its pastors. The Episcopate united

[1] S. John xvi.

to its centre is, in all ages, divinely sustained and divinely assisted to perpetuate and to enunciate the original revelation. It is not my purpose here to offer proof of this assertion. To do so belongs to the treatise *De Ecclesiâ;* but I may note that the promise of the Temporal Mission of the Holy Ghost was made emphatically to the Apostles, and inclusively to the faithful; and emphatically, therefore, to the successors of the Apostles in all ages of the Church. 'He shall give you another Paraclete, who shall abide with you for ever, even the Spirit of Truth.' Again, it was to the Apostles as emphatically, and therefore to their successors with equal emphasis, that our Lord, when He constituted them the sole fountain of His faith and law and jurisdiction to the world, pledged also His perpetual presence and assistance —'all days, even unto the consummation of the world.' And once more, it was to Peter as the head and centre of the Apostles, and for their sakes and for their support in faith, that our Divine Lord said, 'I have prayed for thee, that thy faith fail not, and when thou art converted confirm thy brethren.' It is needless for me to say that the whole tradition of the Fathers recognises the perpetuity of the Apostolic College in the Episcopate diffused throughout the world. S. Irenæus declares it to be anointed with the unction of the truth, alluding to the words of S. John, 'You have the unction from the Holy One, and know all things.' 'And as for you, let the unction which you have received from Him abide in you. And you have no need that any man teach you; but as His unction teacheth you of all things, and is truth, and is no lie. And as it hath taught you, abide in Him.'[1]

And thus the revelation of God is divinely preserved and divinely proposed to the world. A Divine revelation in human custody is soon lost; a Divine revelation expounded by human interpreters, or enunciated by human discernment, puts off its Divine character and becomes human, as S. Jerome says of the Scriptures, when perverted by men.

So it might be said of the Church. But God has provided that what He has revealed should be for ever preserved and enunciated by the perpetual presence and assistance of the same Spirit from whom the revelation originally came. And this gives us the basis of divine certainty and the rule of divine faith.

(1) The voice of the living Church of this hour, when it declares what God has revealed is no other than the voice of the Holy Spirit, and therefore

---

[1] 1 S. John ii. 20-27.

generates divine faith in those who believe. The Baptismal Creed represents at this day, in all the world, the preaching of the Apostles and the faith of Pentecost. It is the voice of the same Divine Teacher who spoke in the beginning, enunciating now the same truth in the same words.

(2) Holy Scripture, known to be such, and rightly understood, is certainly the voice of the Holy Ghost, and likewise may generate acts of Divine faith.

(3) Whatsoever Tradition is found in all the world, neither written in Scripture nor decreed by any Council of the Church, but running up beyond the Scripture and the General Councils, is, according to S. Augustine's rule, certainly of Divine origin.[1]

(4) The Decrees of General Councils are undoubtedly the voice of the Holy Ghost, both because they are the organs of the active infallibility of the Church, and because they have the pledge of a special divine assistance according to the needs of the Church and of the Faith.

(5) The Definitions and Decrees of Pontiffs, speaking *ex cathedrâ,* or as the Head of the Church and to the whole Church, whether by Bull, or Apostolic

---

[1] 'Quod universa tenet Ecclesia, nec conciliis institutum, sed semper retentum est, non nisi auctoritate apostolica traditum rectissime creditur.'—S. Aug. *De Bapt. cont. Donat.* lib. iv. 31, tom. ix. p. 140.

Letters, or Encyclical, or Brief, to many or to one person, undoubtedly emanate from a divine assistance, and are infallible.

S. Augustine argues as follows of the Head and the body: 'Therefore as the soul animates and quickens our whole body, but perceives in the head by the action of life, by hearing, by smelling, by the taste, and by touch, in the other members by touch alone (for all are subject to the head in their operation, the head being placed above them for their guidance, since the head bears the personality of the soul itself, which guides the body, for there all the senses are manifested), so to the whole people of the saints, as of one body, the man Christ Jesus, the Mediator between God and man, is head.'[1]

Now the Pontiffs, as Vicars of Jesus Christ, have a twofold relation, the one to the Divine Head of the Church of whom they are the representatives on earth, the other to the whole body. And these two relations

---

[1] 'Quomodo ergo anima totum corpus nostrum animat et vivificat, sed in capite et vivendo sentit et audiendo et odorando et gustando et tangendo, in ceteris autem membris tangendo tantum; et ideo capiti cuncta subjecta sunt ad operandum, illud autem supra collocatum est ad consulendum; quia ipsius animae, quae consulit corpori, quodam modo personam sustinet caput, ibi enim omnis sensus apparet: sic universo populo sanctorum tanquam uni corpori caput est Mediator Dei et hominum homo Christus Jesus.'—S. Aug. *De Agone Christ.* cap. 22, tom. vi. p. 254.

impart a special prerogative of grace to him that bears them. The endowments of the head, as S. Augustine argues, are in behalf of the body. It is a small thing to say that the endowments of the body are the prerogatives of the head. The Vicar of Jesus Christ would bear no proportion to the body if, while it is infallible, he were not. He would bear also no representative character if he were the fallible witness of an infallible Head. Though the analogy observed by S. Augustine between the head and the members cannot strictly apply to the Vicar of Christ and the members upon earth, nevertheless it invests him with a pre-eminence of guidance and direction over the whole body, which can neither be possessed by any other member of the body, nor by the whole body without him, and yet attaches to him personally and alone as representing to the body the prerogatives of its Divine Head. The infallibility of the Head of the Church extends to the whole matter of revelation, that is, to the Divine truth and the Divine law, and to all those facts or truths which are in contact with faith and morals. The definitions of the Church include truths of the natural order, and the revelation of supernatural truth is in contact with natural ethics, politics, and philosophy. The doctrines of the consubstantiality of the Son, of transubstantiation, and of the constitution of humanity, touch upon truths of philosophy and of the natural order, but being in contact with the faith, they fall within the infallibility of the Church. So again the judgments of Pontiffs in matters which affect the welfare of the whole Church, such as the condemnation of propositions. In all declarations that such propositions are, as the case may be, heretical or savouring of heresy, or erroneous, or scandalous, or offensive to pious ears, and the like, the assistance of the Holy Spirit certainly preserves the Pontiffs from error; and such judgments are infallible, and demand interior assent from all.

(6) The unanimous voice of the Saints in any matter of the Divine truth or law can hardly be believed to be other than the voice of the Spirit of God by the rule, 'Consensus Sanctorum sensus Spiritûs Sancti est.'[1]

And though there is no revealed pledge of infallibility to the Saints as such, yet the consent of the

---

[1] 'Quinta igitur conclusio est. In conclusione sacrarum litterarum communis omnium sanctorum veterum intelligentia certissimum argumentum theologo praestat ad theologicas assertiones corroborandas; quippe cum sanctorum omnium sensus Spiritus Sancti sensus ipse sit.'—Melchior Canus, *De Locis Theol., de Sanct. Auct.* lib. vii. cap. 3, concl. 5.

Saints is a high test of what is the mind and illumination of the Spirit of Truth.

(7) The voice of Doctors, when simply delivering the dogma of the Church, is identified with the voice of the Church, and partakes of its certainty. But in commenting on it they speak as private men, and their authority is human.

(8) The voice of the Fathers has weight as that of Saints and of Doctors, and also as witnesses to the faith in the ages in which they lived, and yet they cannot generate divine faith nor afford a divine certainty. As S. Gregory the Great says: 'Doctores Fidelium discipulos Ecclesiæ.' They are taught by the Church; and the judgment of a Council or a Pontiff is generically distinct from the witness or judgment of any number of Fathers, and is of a higher order, and emanates from a special assistance.

(9) The authority of Philosophers is still more evidently fallible, because more simply human.

(10) The authority of Human Histories is more uncertain still, and can afford no adequate motive of divine certainty.

(11) The Reason or Private Judgment of individuals exercised critically upon history, philosophy, theology, Scripture, and revelation, inasmuch as it is the most human, is also the most fallible and uncer-

tain of all principles of faith, and cannot in truth be rightly described to be such. Yet this is ultimately all that remains to those who reject the infallibility of the living Church.

In conclusion, if the relation between the body and the Spirit be conditional and dissoluble, then the enunciations of the Church are fallible and subject to human criticism.

If the relation be absolute and indissoluble, then all its enunciations by Pontiffs, Councils, Traditions, Scriptures, and universal consent of the Church, are divine, and its voice also is divine, and identified with the voice of its Divine Head in heaven.

But that the relation between the body and the Spirit is absolute and indissoluble, the Theologians, Fathers, Scriptures, and the universal Church, as we have seen above, declare.

And therefore the infallibility of the Church is perpetual, and the truths of revelation are so enunciated by the Church as to anticipate all research, and to exclude from their sphere all human criticism.

CHAPTER II.

THE RELATION OF THE HOLY GHOST TO THE HUMAN REASON.

In the last chapter I have, I trust, established the indissolubility of the union between the Holy Spirit and the Holy Catholic Church; from which follows, by necessity, its perpetual infallibility, both active and passive. I have indicated, at least in outline, the organs through which that infallibility is exercised, and have noted the degrees of authority possessed by them, and the kind and degrees of assent required by the acts and words of the Church or of its members.

In the present chapter I purpose to trace out the relation of the Holy Spirit to the reason of man, both the collective reason of the Church and the individual reason of its members taken one by one.

Now, there are two ways in which the relation of the Holy Spirit delivering the revelation of God to the human reason may be treated.

1. First, we might consider the relation of reve-

lation to reason in those who as yet do not believe; that is, in the examination of evidence to establish the fact of a revelation, and to ascertain its nature.

2. Secondly, the relation of revelation to reason after the fact has been accepted.

In the first case the reason acts as a judge of evidence, in the second it submits as a disciple to a Divine Teacher.

In the former case the reason must, by necessity, act as a judge in estimating the motives of credibility. Adults in every age become Christian upon being convinced by the proper evidence that Christianity is a divine revelation. This process of reason is the preamble of faith. Once illuminated, the reason of man becomes the disciple of a Divine Teacher.

Such was the state of those who in the beginning came as adults to Christianity. Now they are the exceptions in Christendom. The rule of God's dealings is that revelation should be, not a discovery, but an inheritance. To illustrate my meaning I may say—Adult baptism was at first the rule, now it is the exception; Infant baptism is the rule of God's dealing with us. So we inherit revelation before we examine it; and faith anticipates judgment. Again, to state the same in other words, there are two ways of considering the relation of reason to revelation, the one according to the logical and the other the historical order.

S. Thomas treats it in the logical order. He says that science or rational knowledge is useful and necessary to faith in four ways: (1) Faith presupposes the operations of reason on the motives of credibility for which we believe. (2) Faith is rendered intrinsically credible by reason. (3) Faith is illustrated by reason. (4) Faith is defended by reason against the sophisms of false philosophy.[1]

It will perhaps be easier if we take the historical order, because it follows more simply the method of God's dealing with us. We will therefore treat first of the rule, and hereafter, so far as needs be, of the exceptions.

I speak then of the relations of reason to revelation in those who are within the light and tradition of truth.

I. The first relation of reason to revelation is to receive it by intellectual apprehension. It is like

[1] 'E veramente l' Angelico ha costantemente inculcato la necessità ed utilità della scienza per riguardo alla Fede, e le ha dedotte da quattro capi, i quali sono questi: la Fede presuppone la scienza, si rende credibile per la scienza, è illustrata in qualche modo con la scienza, e dalla scienza vien difesa contra i sofismi della falsa filosofia.'—Sanseverino, *I Principali Sistemi della Filosofia sul Criterio*, Napoli, 1858, p. 14.

the relation of the eye to the light. There are, I may say, two kinds of sight, the passive and the active; that is, in plain words, there is a difference between seeing and looking. In the former the will is quiescent, in the latter it is in activity. We see a thousand things when we look only at one; we see the light even when we do not consciously fix the eye upon any particular object by an act of the will. So the intellect is both passive and active. And the intellect must first be in some degree passively replenished or illuminated by an object before it can actively apply itself to it. What is this but to go back to our old lessons in logic, to the three primary operations of the mind—apprehension, judgment, and discourse or process of reasoning? Now the apprehension of our logic is what may be called the passive relation of the reason to revelation, by which it apprehends, or understands, or knows, call it which we will, the meaning or outline of the truth presented to it before as yet it has made any act either of judgment or of discourse.

And this may be said to be the normal and most perfect relation of the reason to revelation. It is the nearest approach which can be made in this world to the quiescent contemplation of truth. It is the state into which we return after the most prolonged and active process of the intellect; the state to which we ascend by the most perfect operations of reasoning. The degrees of explicit knowledge deepen the intensity of knowledge; but the difference of knowing God as a child and knowing God as a philosopher is not in kind but in degree of discursive knowledge, and the knowledge of the philosopher may be less perfect than the knowledge of the child.

The proof of this appears to be evident. Revelation is not discovery, or rather revelation is the discovery of Himself by God to man, not by man for himself. It is not the activity of the human reason which discovers the truths of revelation. It is God discovering or withdrawing the veil from His own intelligence, and casting the light of it upon us. These are truisms; but they are truths almost as universally forgotten and violated in the common habits of thought as they are universally admitted when enunciated.

We may take an illustration from science. Astronomy is a knowledge which comes to us by discovery. It was built up by active observation, and by reasoning. A tradition of astronomy has descended to us from the highest antiquity, perpetually expanding its circumference and including new regions of truth. But its whole structure is the result of the active reason. Even star-gazing is an active process of search. Chemistry again is still more a science of discovery, of experiment, of conjecture, and of active inquiry after secret qualities in minerals, vegetables, gases, and the like. Hardly any part of it can be said to be self-evident, or to anticipate discovery. Much more all the truths which come by the application of science, by the crossing, as it were, of the races and families of truths in the natural world.

All these branches and provinces of human knowledge may be called discoveries, not revelations. They are the fruits of an intense, prolonged, and accumulated cultivation of the human reason, and of the distinct soil of subject-matter of each region of truth.

Such may be called the genesis of science. But the relation of science to revelation is not our subject. I speak of it only to show the difference between the relation of reason to natural science and to revelation, and so dismiss it. When we come to revelation, the process of the reason is inverted. We start from a knowledge which we have not discovered, which we passively received, which we may cultivate for ever without enlarging its circumference or multiplying the articles of faith.

It is impossible to quote Scripture without seeming to use it in proof. But I quote it now, not as proof, but only as the best formula to express my meaning, which must be proved indeed by other proper reasons.

First, then, though the existence of God may be proved by reason and from lights of the natural order, it is certain that the knowledge of God's existence anticipated all such reasoning. The theism of the world was not a discovery. Mankind possessed it by primeval revelation, was penetrated and pervaded by it before any doubted of it, and reasoning did not precede but follow the doubts. Theists came before Philosophers, and Theism before Atheism, or even a doubt about the existence of God.[1] S. Paul says that 'the invisible things of Him from the creation of the world are clearly *seen*, being understood by the things which are made, His eternal power also and divinity, so that they are inexcusable.'[2] The word *seen* signifies that God reflects Himself from the face of His works, and that the

[1] 'Deinde dato, quod metaphysicè contingere possit omnimoda Dei ignorantia invincibilis in eo, qui peccat, ut proinde metaphysicè dari possit peccatum pure Philosophicum: Nihilominus de facto est moraliter impossibilis isthæc ignorantia, qua excusetur homo a reatu odii Divini, et pœnæ æternæ, dum ponit humano modo actum graviter disconvenientem naturæ rationali, ac rationis dictamini; unde peccatum pure Philosophicum est saltem moraliter in præsenti providentia impossibile. Ratio est, quia in præsenti providentia non datur ignorantia Dei invincibilis in hominibus ratione utentibus. Viva, *Theses Damnatæ. Prop. de Peccato Philosophico ab Alex. VIII. damn.* pars iii. p. 13, sec. 12.

[2] Rom. i. 20.

human intelligence, which was illuminated with the traditional knowledge of God, could read by reasoning the proofs of His existence in that reflection. These primary truths, therefore, of natural theology are propounded by the visible world to the reason of man. The knowledge of the existence of God pervaded the human intelligence as a traditional axiom, an inherited light, a consciousness of the human family anterior to all reflections upon the proofs, or analysis of the evidence from which it springs. The alleged instances of individuals and races without the knowledge of God are anomalies in the history of mankind, and errors in philosophy.

What is true of natural is still more true of revealed theology. The knowledge which God has discovered of Himself came to man by gift and by infusion, not by logic nor by research. 'God who at sundry times and in divers manners hath spoken to us in time past by the prophets, has in these last days spoken to us by His Son.'[1] 'The Word was made flesh and dwelt among us, and we beheld His glory, the glory as of the only-begotten of the Father, full of grace and truth.' 'God, who commanded the light to shine out of darkness, hath shined in our hearts.'[2]

The Incarnation was the revelation of God by per-

---

[1] Heb. i. 1.   [2] S. John i. 14; 2 Cor. iv. 6.

sonal manifestation and immediate illumination of the human reason. The Disciples knew Him gradually, not by gradual processes of discovery, but by gradual revelation of Himself. The light of 'the face of Jesus Christ' was the source of their illumination. As He gradually revealed Himself by His miracles, His words, His passion, His resurrection, His ascension, their apprehension of His Godhead and His power enlarged its circle, and their consciousness of His Divine personality and power pervaded all their intellect with the evidence of a supernatural light. What Jesus was to His Disciples the Holy Spirit was still further to the Apostles. The day of Pentecost filled up the whole outline of the revelation of which Jesus was both the subject and the first Discoverer, that is, Revealer to the human reason.

But these are self-evident truths. The collective intelligence of the Apostles was the centre and springhead of the collective intelligence of the Church. The Church is composed of head, body, soul, intelligence, and will; and the illumination of truth pervades it in all its faculties, and sustains in it a perpetual consciousness of the whole outline of revelation. All that Jesus revealed in person or by His Spirit hangs suspended in the mind of the Church. It was not discovered by it, but revealed to it, and received by the quiescent intellect, which thereby was illuminated by a divine light. Its activity was elicited by the infusion of revealed truth, and the intelligence of the Church apprehended and comprehended by an active knowledge the revelation it had received.

And thus truth became an inheritance, descending from generation to generation, anticipating all discovery, search, or doubt, and filling the intelligence with its light, taking possession of it by a divine operation. It is sustained indeed by the presence of a Divine Person and an infallible Teacher. But this latter point does not enter at present into the matter before us, which is to consider of the relations of the reason in individuals, or of the faithful as a body, to the deposit of revelation, and not the relations of the 'magisterium Ecclesiæ,' or of the operation of the reason of the Church under the assistance and as the organ of an infallible Teacher. This would need a separate treatment, and involve another class and series of questions, and must be reserved for another place.

II. The second relation of the reason to revelation is to propagate the truth it has received. 'Go ye and make disciples of all nations.'[1] 'Freely have

[1] S. Matt. xxviii. 19.

ye received, freely give.'[1] They were the messengers of a Divine Teacher, the witnesses of an order of divine facts. The reason of the Apostles diffused what it had received. They enumerated what they had learned, not as discoveries—nor as conclusions of dialectics—nor as philosophies—nor as criticisms —but as declarations of the Divine mind and will. 'The Jews require signs, and the Greeks seek after wisdom: but we preach Christ crucified, unto the Jews indeed a stumbling-block, and unto the Gentiles foolishness; but unto them that are called, both Jews and Greeks, Christ the power of God and the wisdom of God.'[2]

The reason of mankind, in like manner, received the revelation declared to it both by the lights of nature and by the lights of Pentecost. 'I was found of them that did not seek me; I appeared openly to them that asked not after me.'[3]

The preaching of the Apostles was an affirmation of truth; not as a problem to be proved, but as a revelation to be believed. As when our Divine Lord said 'Search the Scriptures,' He did not rest the proof of His own Divine personality, mission, and truth upon the private judgment of His hearers; so

---

[1] S. Matt. x. 8. [2] 1 Cor. i. 22, 24.
[3] Isaias in Rom. x. 20.

the Apostles, when they preached Jesus at Berœa or at Athens, referred their hearers to Scripture and to nature, not as if their preaching depended upon these, but because their preaching was the key and fulfilment of the meaning both of Scripture and of nature. What they had apprehended from the lips of a Divine Teacher, they declared in His name to the apprehension of other men; and in this tradition of truth from intelligence to intelligence, the reason in its quiescent apprehension was filled with an absolute certainty which anticipated all inquiry. The searching of Scriptures added nothing objectively to the light and certainty of the truth delivered to them. It only assured them subjectively that what the Apostles taught was what nature and Scripture taught likewise, so far as they extended. To the Athenians S. Paul was a babbler and a word-sower, and Jesus and the Resurrection were strange gods, till they believed the Apostle to be a teacher sent from God. They then believed not anything they had discovered, but what they heard.

III. A third relation of reason to revelation is to define the truths divinely presented to it. What was apprehended was immediately clothed in words. The intellect invests its thoughts in words as it apprehends them. The illumination of the day of

Pentecost found utterance at once in many tongues. It clothed itself in the words of many languages; and those words certainly were not chosen without the assistance of the same Divine Teacher who revealed the truths which they expressed. The first definitions of the Christian Faith are the Articles of the Baptismal Creed. We may pass over the historical traditions of the time and place of its first compositions. It is enough for our purpose to say, that the same doctrines, in the same order, and, so far as the diversity of language admits, in the same words, were delivered to the catechumens and to the baptized throughout the world. In S. Irenæus, Tertullian, Origen, S. Cyprian, and S. Gregory Thaumaturgus, the outline of this universal creed may be read. The Churches of Cæsarea, Jerusalem, Antioch, Alexandria, in the East; of Rome, Aquileia, Ravenna and Tours, of Gaul, Africa, and Spain, in the West, taught them in the same terms and order. In S. Cyril of Jerusalem in the East, and in S. Nicetas in the West, the Baptismal Creed may be found expounded. In the Councils of Nice and Constantinople it was more explicitly declared. In all this, the reason of the Church defined by a reflex act, the truths of which it was possessed.

Again: the Church in its General Councils has

lineally defined the original revelation according to the needs of each successive age. The eighteen General Councils are one continuous action of the same mind, preserving the identity of truth, and defining it by a growing precision of expression.

In like manner, the theology of the Church consists chiefly in an enunciation of revealed truths. Its dialectical, or polemical, processes are not its primary operations. S. John, who is called the Theologian, may be taken as a type of the sacred science. The heavens were opened to him, and the throne and the heavenly court, the history and future of the Church were revealed. What he saw he fixed in words. What was visible in the heavens he transcribed upon the page of the Apocalypse. It was a process of apprehension and description, by which the structure and action of the kingdom of God in heaven and earth was delineated.

Such, in its primary operation, is the nature of theology, which defines and enunciates the divine truths and facts of revelation, and presents them in their manifold unity, symmetry, and relations, and that in three distinct spheres or circles of truth: first, the original Revelation; secondly, the definitions framed of apostolical tradition, of pontiffs, and of councils; and thirdly, the judgments and dogmatic facts, in which the Church speaks infallibly.

In all this the reason is as a disciple who intelligently apprehends, rehearses, and defines the truths which he has received.

IV. A fourth relation of reason to revelation is to defend it. And this may be in two ways, negatively and positively.

By negatively I mean that the reason can demonstrate the nullity of arguments brought against revelation, either by showing their intrinsic invalidity, or by the analogy of the facts of nature. But in this process the reason does not assume to demonstrate the truth of revealed doctrines, which rest upon their own proper evidence. It is reason against reason. Reason contending for revelation against reason contending against it. All the while revelation stands upon its own basis, that is the natural and supernatural witness, or consciousness and illumination of the Church. The argument against objectors simply clears away what may be called the criticism or rationalism of the human reason opposing itself to the revelation of the Divine.

The positive defence of theology occupies itself with demonstrating the possibility of revelation, its fitness, its probability, the necessity of a revelation, and the fact.

The first and simplest form of this defensive operation of the reason is to be found in the ancient Apologies, such as those of Justin Martyr, Tertullian, Arnobius, Minucius Felix, in which the possibility, probability, and fitness of revelation are assumed, and the whole effort of the apologists is directed to prove the fact, and that Christianity is that revelation. But this is addressed not to those who are within the Church, but to those who are without; that is, to Jews and Gentiles.

In these Apologies we find the simple enunciation of the doctrines of faith, but no system or method of theological science.

It is remarkable how little trace of scientific theology is to be found in the Oriental Church. Exuberant as it was in expositions of Holy Scripture, and in dogmatic treatises on the mysteries in controversy during the period of the four first General Councils, of which the Commentaries of Origen and S. John Chrysostom, and the works of S. Athanasius, S. Gregory of Nyssa, S. Gregory of Nazianzum, S. Basil, and S. Cyril of Alexandria, are witness, nevertheless there is hardly to be traced any attempt at a theological method or complete scientific expression of revelation. Dialectical, exact, and positive as S. Augustine is, it cannot be said that a scientific method of theology is to be found in his works. Some theologians are of opinion, that traces of such a scientific treatment are to be found in the writings of Theophilus of Antioch, Clement of Alexandria, S. Cyril of Jerusalem, Lactantius, and others; but in truth the first writer in whom anything of scientific arrangement or completeness of method is to be found is S. John of Damascus in the eighth century. And it may be said that his work, 'De Orthodoxa Fide,' is both the first and the last to be found in the Oriental Church, so stationary and unreflective, it would seem, has the Oriental mind become since its separation from the centre of spiritual and intellectual activity, the Chair of S. Peter. Since S. John of Damascus, I hardly know what the Greek Church has produced, except a few meagre Catenas of the Fathers upon certain books of Holy Scripture, the works of Theophylact, a body of miserable Erastian canon law, a few still more meagre catechetical works, and many virulent and schismatical attacks upon the Primacy of the Holy See. It may be truly said that the history of the human intellect in the last eighteen hundred years is the history of Christianity, and the history of Christianity is the history of the Catholic Church. It is in the Catholic Church that the human intellect has developed its activity and its maturity, both within the sphere of revelation and beyond it.

It was not before the eleventh century that theology assumed a scientific and systematic form. Italy and France may claim the precedence, because the two who led the way in this work were born in, or reared by them; but it is no little glory to England that they were both Archbishops of Canterbury, Lanfranc and his disciple S. Anselm. It was another Archbishop of Canterbury who gave to the theological studies of England a scientific direction by introducing into the University of Oxford the study of Aristotle; which, strange to say, endures to this day—I mean S. Edmund. After these came Hugh and Richard of S. Victor, Hildebert of Tours, Robert Pool, Otto of Frisingen, S. Bernard, and others. It was at this period that the first explicit collision took place between reason ministering to revelation as its disciple, and reason dissecting it as a critic; that is, between S. Bernard and Abelard.

There may be said to be three epochs in the science of theology.

S. Anselm is not untruly thought to be the first who gave to theology the scientific impulse which has stamped a new form and method on its treatment. His two works, the 'Cur Deus Homo,' or 'Ratio Incarnationis,' and that on the Holy Trinity called 'Fides quærens Intellectum Divinæ Essentiæ et SSmæ Trinitatis,' may be said to mark the first of the three epochs in theological science. The chief axiom of S. Anselm's theological method may be expressed in his own words : 'Sicut rectus ordo exigit ut profunda Christianæ fidei prius credamus quam ea præsumamus ratione discutere, ita negligentia mihi videtur, si postquam confirmati sumus in fide, non studemus quod credimus intelligere.'[1]

The second epoch was constituted by the 'Liber Sententiarum' of Peter Lombard, which formed the text of the Schools for nearly two centuries. Alexander of Hales, Albertus Magnus, S. Bonaventura, S. Thomas, and many more commented on the Book of the Sentences, and formed the School of the Sententiastæ, who were fated to pass away before the greater light of the third epoch.

The third epoch was made by S. Thomas. It is indeed true that England may claim somewhat of this glory. Before the Summa Theologica of S. Thomas, Alexander of Hales had formed a Summa Universæ Theologiæ, which would have inaugurated

---

[1] *Cur Deus Homo*, lib. i. c. 2.

a new period, had not the more perfect amplitude, order, and unity of S. Thomas cast all others into shade. From this time the Book of the Sentences gave way to the Sum of Theology as the text of the Schools, and the Sententiastæ yielded to the Summistæ. From this time onward two great streams of scientific theology flow towards us, the one of Dominican commentators on the Sum of their great doctor, such as Caietan, Sylvius, the Sotos, and others; the other, which sprang later, of Jesuit commentators, Suarez, Vasquez, De Lugo, and the like.

Since the Council of Trent, another mode of treating theology has arisen. The controversy with the pretended appeal to antiquity, threw the Catholic theologian more and more upon the study of the History of Dogma; and theology assumed what is called the positive method. Nevertheless, the Scholastic method still held and holds to this day its ascendency. And that because it represents the intellectual process of the Church, elaborating, through a period of many centuries, an exact conception and expression of revealed truth. The Scholastic method can never cease to be true, just as logic can never cease to be true, because it is the intellectual order of revealed truths in their mutual relations, harmony, and unity. To depreciate it is to show that we do not understand it. The critical and exegetical studies which are tributary to it may be advanced and corrected, but the form of the Scholastic theology has its basis in the intrinsic nature and relations of the truths of which it treats. All else is subordinate and accidental.

V. The last relation of which I will speak is that of transmitting theology by a scientific treatment and tradition. The mind or intelligence of the Church has had, as we have seen, many relations to the revelation entrusted to it, namely, that of passive reception, from which arises the consciousness of supernatural knowledge;—that of enunciation, which presupposes apprehension or conception of the truths received;—that of definition, or the precise verbal expression, and the orderly digest of the doctrines of faith;—that of defence, by way of proof and evidence;—and, finally, by a scientific treatment and tradition. I say scientific, because theology, though not a science *propriè dictu*, may be truly and correctly so described.

The definition of Science, according to both philosophers and theologians, is 'the habit of the mind conversant with necessary truth,' that is, truth which admits of demonstration and of the certainty which excludes the possibility of its contradictory being true. According to the Scholastic philosophy, Science is defined as follows:—

Viewed *subjectively*, it is 'The certain and evident knowledge of the ultimate reasons or principles of truth, attained by reasoning.'

Viewed *objectively*, it is 'The system of known truths belonging to the same order, as a whole, and depending upon one only principle.' [1]

This is founded on the definition of Aristotle. In the sixth book of the Ethics, ch. 3, he says: 'From this it is evident what Science is; to speak accurately, and not to follow mere similitudes, for we all understand that what we know cannot be otherwise than we know it. For whatsoever may or may not be, as a practical question, is not known to be or not to be. For that which is known is necessary; therefore eternal. For whatsoever is necessary is simply eternal.' [2]

---

[1] 'Essa [la scienza] viene considerata sotto un doppio rispetto, l'uno oggettivo, e l'altro subbiettivo; per il primo essa significa un *sistema intiero di cognizioni dimostrate e dipendenti da un solo principio*, come gli anelli di una stessa catena; per il secondo si definisce: *una cognizione certa ed evidente delle ultime ragioni delle cose ottenuta mercè del ragionamento.*'—Sanseverino, *Elementi di Filosofia Speculativa*, vol. i. pp. 130, 131. Napoli, 1862.

[2] Ἐπιστήμη μὲν οὖν τί ἐστιν, ἐντεῦθεν φανερὸν εἰ δεῖ ἀκριβολογεῖσθαι καὶ μὴ ἀκολουθεῖν ταῖς ὁμοιότησιν. Πάντες γὰρ ὑπολαμβάνομεν, ὃ ἐπιστάμεθα, μὴ ἐνδέχεσθαι ἄλλως ἔχειν· τὰ δ' ἐνδεχόμενα ἄλλως, ὅταν ἔξω τοῦ θεωρεῖν γένηται, λανθάνει εἰ ἔστιν ἢ μή. Ἐξ ἀνάγκης ἄρα ἐστὶ τὸ ἐπιστητόν. Arist. *Ethics*, book vi. chap. iii.

Such also is the definition of S. Thomas, who says, 'Whatsoever truths are truly known, as by certain knowledge (ut certa scientia), are known by resolution into their first principles, which of themselves are immediately present to the intellect; and so all science is constituted by a vision of the thing as present, so that it is impossible that the same thing should be the object both of faith and of science, because, that is, of the obscurity of the principles of faith.'[1] Nevertheless, he affirms that from principles accepted by faith, truths may be proved to the faithful, as from principles naturally known to others; and that, therefore, theology is a science:[2] but this, as Vasquez shows from Caietan, is to be understood not simply, but relatively—*non simpliciter, sed secundum quid.* The opinion of Caietan, founded on S. Thomas, is, that

[1] 'Quæcumque sciuntur propriè, ut certa scientia, cognoscuntur per resolutionem in prima principia, quæ per se præsto sunt intellectui; et sic omnis scientia in visione rei præsentis perficitur: unde impossibile est, quod de eodem sit fides et scientia.'—D. Thom. *De Veritate*, quæst. xiv. art. 9.

[2] 'Respondeo. Dicendum, Sacram Doctrinam esse scientiam. Sed sciendum est, quod duplex est scientiarum genus. Quædam enim sunt, quæ procedunt ex principiis notis lumine naturali intellectus, sicut Arithmetica, Geometria, et hujusmodi. Quædam vero sunt, quæ procedunt ex principiis notis lumine superioris scientiæ: sicut Perspectiva procedit ex principiis notificatis per Geometriam; et Musica ex principiis per Arithmeticam notis. Et hoc modo Sacra Doctrina est scientia, quia procedit ex principiis notis lumine superioris scientiæ, quæ scilicet est scientia Dei et Beatorum.'—D. Thom. *Sum. Theol.* Prima pars, quæst. i. art. 2.

theology is to be understood in two ways—as it is in itself, and as it is in us. The former is as it is in God and the blessed, which is properly science; the latter, as it is in us, as 'viatores,' in which state it is a science subalternate, deriving its principles from the science in God by faith, and therefore not to be called properly a science.[1] The Thomists generally seem to have held ' that theology in us, as " viatores," when deduced from articles known by divine faith only, is true and proper science, not only in itself, but as it is in us; but, nevertheless, *imperfect in its kind.*' But the more common opinion among the Scholastic theologians affirms that theology in us, 'viatores,' as it is in us, is not true and proper science. Such is the opinion also of Vasquez, and of many quoted by him.

The summary of the question is given by Gregory of Valentia, who says : ' That theology is not science

[1] 'Bifariam ergo Caietanus accipit Theologiam : unam dicit esse Dei et Beatorum ; alteram vero viatorum ; hanc posteriorem rursus dividit in Theologiam secundum se, et prout est in nobis. . . . . Asserit igitur in viatoribus esse imperfectam scientiam, hoc est, non vere et proprie scientiam sed scientiam subalternatam

' Quarta sententia [opinio Alberti et Thomistarum] satis communis inter recentiores est, Theologiam viatorum ex articulis sola fide divina creditis deductam esse vere et proprie scientiam, non tantum secundum se sed etiam ut est in ipsis viatoribus, imperfectam tamen in suo genere.

'Ultima igitur sententia magis communis inter Scholasticos affirmat Theologiam viatorum ut in ispis est, non esso vere et proprie scientiam.'—Vasquez, *Disp. in l. c. D. Thom.* vol. i. pp. 10, 11.

is taught by Durandus, Ocham, Gabriel, and others, whose opinions I hold to be the truest. The foundation of all these is most certain, namely, that it is of the essence of science, according to Aristotle, that the assent elicited by it should be evident; for he who *knows*, must know that the thing cannot be otherwise than he knows it to be. But the habit of theology does not elicit such an assent. For theological assent must be resolved into two, or at least one proposition resting on faith, which cannot be evident. Therefore, theological assent is not evident. . . . . But this does not detract from the dignity of theology. For though it be not a proper science, it is a habit absolutely more perfect than any science.'

Gregory of Valentia goes on to say, ' Let theology, then, be neither science in itself—as the philosophers describe it —nor properly a science subalternated to the science of God and of the blessed, but only *improprie*, by reason of a certain similitude which it bears to sciences which are properly subalternated to higher sciences, because it proceeds from the assertions of faith, or from principles which are known by the knowledge and science of God and of the blessed. Yet nevertheless by the best of rights it may be called a science, because, absolutely, it is a habit more perfect than any science described by philosophers.'

Gregory of Valentia proceeds to show that theology is more perfect than science properly so called. He does so by affirming that it is wisdom. This he proves by showing that it has the 'three conditions of wisdom. First, it treats of the highest and universal truths. Secondly, it is so called in Scripture. Thirdly, it may be proved to be so by the authority of Aristotle; because the five conditions required by him in wisdom, and found by him in metaphysics—the highest wisdom in his esteem—are fulfilled in an eminent degree by theology.' First, it deals with universals. Second, with things the most removed from sense. Third, it is a most certain habit of the intellect, proceeding from the most certain causes. Fourth, it is self-caused, and not caused by any other science. Fifth, it is directed by no other science, but directs itself and all other sciences.[1]

'Theology, then,' as Vasquez says, 'does not mean

[1] 'Theologiam igitur non esse proprie scientiam talem, qualem Aristoteles descripsit, docent Durandus, Arimin., Ocham, Gabriel. Marsil., et alii, quorum sententiam puto verissimam. Fundamentum enim horum omnium est certissimum, nempe quod de ratione scientiæ secundum Arist. est, ut assensus ab ea elicitus sit evidens: cum oporteat, eum qui scit, cognoscere, non posse rem aliter se habere, atque adeo assentiri immobiliter. Sed habitus Theologiæ non elicit talem assensum. Ergo non est scientia talis, qualis ab Arist. describitur. Assumptio probatur. Nam assensus Theologicus debet resolvi in duas aut saltem in unam propositionem fidei, quæ non est evidens. . . . Nec propterea decedit aliquid de dignitate Theologiæ.

any kind of knowledge of God, for so faith also might be called theology; nor does it mean the knowledge by which we know how to explain and to defend that which is delivered in Scripture: but by theology is understood a science by which, from principles revealed in Scripture, or by the authority of councils, or confirmed and believed by the tradition

Etsi enim propriè scientia non est, est tamen habitus perfectior simpliciter, quàm scientia.

' Maneat ergo Theologiam neque secundum se quidem esse scientiam talem, qualem descripserunt Philosophi, neque propriè scientiam subalternatam scientiæ Dei et Beatorum, sed tantum improprié, propter nonnullam similitudinem, quam habet cum propriè subalternatis, hoc ipso quod procedit ex assertionibus fidei, tanquam ex principiis quæ sunt notæ per scientiam Dei et Beatorum. Et nihilominus tamen optimo jure scientiam appellari, eo quòd est absolutè perfectior habitus, quàm ulla scientia descripta a Philosophis. Theologiam esse sapientiam potest probari, PRIMO, ex ipsa vocis notione. Nam cum Theologia in suo genere consideret res divinas, et certissime, et per altissimum, ac maximè universale principium, per revelationem scilicet divinam, maximè propriè est sapientia. SECUNDO, confirmatur ex phrasi Scripturæ, quæ talem scientiam simpliciter vocat sapientiam, 1 Cor. 2, *Sapientiam loquimur inter perfectos,* et cap. 12, *Alii datur sermo sapientiæ.* TERTIO, probatur auctoritate et exemplo Aristotelis, qui lib. i. Met. habitum scientificum existimat nominandum esse sapientiam, si habeat quinque conditiones, quas habet longè præstantius Theologia, quàm ulla scientia humana. PRIMA conditio est, ut eo habitu cognoscantur omnia quodammodo in universali. SECUNDA, ut circa maximè difficilia, et a sensibus remota versetur. TERTIA, ut sit certissimus habitus procedens ex certissimis causis. QUARTA, ut sit causâ sui, et non alterius scientiæ. QUINTA, ut ab alia scientia non dirigatur, sed dirigat ipse, et judicet scientias alias.'—Greg. De Valentia, tom. i. pp. 22, 32, 44.

of the Church, we infer other truths and conclusions by evident consequence.'[1]

Following the principles here laid down, theology may be called a science. First, because it is a science, if not as to its principles, at least as to its form, method, process, development, and transmission. And because, if its principles are not evident, they are, in all the higher regions of it infallibly certain; and because many of them are the necessary, eternal, and incorruptible truths which, according to Aristotle, generate science.

Revelation, then, contemplated and transmitted in exactness and method, may be called a science and the queen of sciences, the chief of the hierarchy of truth; and it enters and takes the first place in the intellectual system and tradition of the world. It possesses all the qualities and conditions of science so far as its subject-matter admits; namely, certainty, as against doubt, definiteness as against vagueness, harmony as against discordance, unity as against incoherence, progress as against dissolution and stagnation.

---

[1] 'Sed nomine Theologiæ significamus scientiam, qua quis ex principiis in Scripturis revelatis, vel conciliorum auctoritate, aut Ecclesiæ traditione firmatis et creditis, infert alias veritates et conclusiones per evidentem consequentiam.'—Vasquez, *in l. c. D. Thom.* disp. iv. art. ii. cap. 1, tom. i. p. 9.

A knowledge and belief of the existence of God has never been extinguished in the reason of mankind. The polytheisms and idolatries which surrounded it were corruptions of a central and dominant truth which, although obscured, was never lost. And the tradition of this truth was identified with the higher and purer operations of the natural reason, which have been called the intellectual system of the world. The mass of mankind, howsoever debased, were always theists. Atheists, as I have said, were anomalies and exceptions. The theism of the primeval revelation formed the intellectual system of the heathen world. The theism of the patriarchal revelation formed the intellectual system of the Hebrew race. The theism revealed in the incarnation of God has formed the intellectual system of the Christian world. 'Sapientia ædificavit sibi domum.' The science or knowledge of God has built for itself a tabernacle in the intellect of mankind, inhabits it, and abides in it.

The intellectual science of the world finds its perfection in the scientific expression of the theology of faith. But from first to last the reason of man is the disciple, not the critic, of the revelation of God: and the highest science of the human intellect is that which, taking its preamble from the light of nature, begins in faith; and receiving its axioms from faith, expands by the procession of truth from truth.

From what has been said many conclusions follow, which can only be stated now by way of propositions. To discuss them would need many chapters. It is evident—

1. First, that the highest and most perfect operation of the reason in respect to revelation presupposes the reception of revelation by faith, of which the whole structure of scientific theology, and the contemplation of truth by the intellect illuminated by faith, are both example and proof.

2. Secondly, that the highest discursive powers of the reason are developed by revelation, which elevates it from the contemplation of the first principles and axioms of truth in the natural order to a higher and wider sphere, unattainable by the reason without faith.

3. Thirdly, that reason is not the source nor the measure of supernatural truth; nor the test of its intrinsic credibility.[1] This principle has been lately

---

[1] In the Brief of Pius IX. to the Archbishop of Munich the contrary to this is expressly condemned. 'Hinc dubitare nolumus, quin ipsius conventus viri commemoratam veritatem noscentes ac pro fitentes uno eodemque tempore plane rejicere ac reprobare voluerint recentem illam ac præposteram philosophandi rationem, quæ etiamsi

affirmed by Pius IX. in the recent Brief to the Archbishop of Munich.

4. Fourthly, that the Church alone, by Divine illumination and assistance, knows, teaches, and authoritatively imposes belief in matters of revealed truth.

5. Fifthly, that theological science, or the operation of reason and criticism upon revealed truth, does not generate faith; but that faith, through the operations of the illuminated reason, acting as a disciple and not as a critic, generates theological science.

6. Sixthly, that if theology in its highest form may not be properly called science, by reason of the obscurity of its principles; much less may historical and biblical criticism be elevated to the character of science.

7. Seventhly, that to erect historical and biblical criticism, or theology founded on it, into a science which is to form the public opinion of the Church, to control the hierarchy, and to conform to itself even

divinam revelationem veluti historicum factum admittat, tamen ineffabiles veritates ab ipsa divina revelatione propositas humanæ rationis investigationibus supponit, perinde ac si illæ veritates rationi subjectæ essent, vel ratio suis viribus et principiis posset consequi intelligentiam et scientiam omnium supernarum sanctissimæ fidei nostræ veritatum, et mysteriorum, quæ ita supra humanam rationem sunt, ut hæc nunquam effici possit idonea ad illa suis viribus, et ex naturalibus suis principiis intelligenda, aut demonstranda.'—*Litt. Pii P P. IX. ad Archiep. Monac.* Dec. 21, 1863.

the judgment of the Holy See, is to invert the whole order of the Divine procedure which has committed the custody and enunciation of revealed truth to the Church, in its office of witness, judge, and teacher.

8. Eighthly, that the Church, acting judicially and magisterially, is the creator of theological science, and controls it by its decisions, which are infallible.

9. Ninthly, that the converse of this would subordinate the Ecclesia docens to the Ecclesia discens.

10. Tenthly, that this subordination of the objective faith and science of the Ecclesia docens to the subjective faith and science of its individual members is of the nature of Gnosticism, Illuminism, and of Rationalism.

11. Eleventhly, that in the ultimate analysis, this procedure would constitute the critical science of the natural reason as the coordinate test of revealed truth by the side of the supernatural discernment of the Church.

Though I cannot enter upon any of these propositions now, I am unwilling to pass over a passage of remarkable beauty bearing on this principle in the works of S. Francis of Sales.

'In a general council, the controverted points of doctrine are first proposed, and theological arguments are employed to discover the truth. These matters having been discussed, the bishops, and particularly the Pope who is their head, conclude and decree what is to be believed; and as soon as they have pronounced, all acquiesce fully in their decision. We must observe, that this submission is not founded on the reasons which have been alleged in the preceding argument, but on the authority of the Holy Ghost, who, presiding invisibly at the council, has concluded, determined, and decreed by the mouth of His ministers, whom He has established pastors of the Church. The arguments and discussions are carried on in the porch; but the decision and acquiescence, by which they are terminated, take place in the sanctuary, where the Holy Spirit specially resides, animating the body of the Church, and speaking by the mouth of the bishops, according to the promise of the Son of God.'[1]

12. Twelfthly, that if coordinate, unless submissive, the critical reason makes itself superior.

13. Thirteenthly, that the superior test is ultimately the sole test of truth, which would be thereby placed in what is called the scientific reason, that is to say, of individuals.

14. Fourteenthly, that the scientific reason would be thereby constituted as the ultimate measure and

[1] S. Francis of Sales, *Treatise on the Love of God*, b. ii. c. xiv.

source of truth, which is pure Rationalism, of which the method laid down in the work called 'Essays and Reviews' is the most recent example among us.

I conclude, then, as I began, that the reason is the disciple, not the critic, of revelation; and that the relation of docility to divine light and to a divine guide is not only consistent with the elevation and development of the human intellect, but the true and only condition of its highest powers and of its scientific perfection. And of this the intellectual history and state of Christendom is evidence. I cannot better express my meaning than by words used on the same subject on another occasion:—

'In a word, it is not science which generates faith, but faith which generates science by the aid of the reason illuminated by revelation. In what I have hitherto said, I have assumed one truth as undeniable and axiomatic, namely, that God has revealed Himself; that He has committed this revelation to His Church; and that He preserves both His revelation and His Church in all ages by His own presence and assistance from all error in faith and morals. Now, inasmuch as certain primary truths— which may be naturally known of God and the soul, and of the relations of the soul with God, and of man with man; that is, certain truths discoverable also in the order of nature by reason or by philosophy—are taken up into and incorporated with the revelation of God, the Church, therefore, possesses the first principles of rational philosophy and of natural ethics, both for individuals and for society. And, inasmuch as these principles are the great regulating truths of philosophy and natural morality, including natural politics, the Church has a voice, a testimony, and a jurisdiction within these provinces of natural knowledge. I do not affirm the Church to be a philosophical authority, but I may affirm it to be a witness in philosophy. Much more when we come to treat of Christian philosophy or the Theodicæa, or Christian morals and Christian politics; for these are no more than the truths of nature grafted upon the stock of revelation, and elevated to a supernatural perfection. To exclude the discernment and voice of the Church from philosophy and politics, is to degrade both by reducing them to the natural order. First, it pollards them, and next, it deprives them of the corroboration of a higher evidence. Against this the whole array of Catholic theologians and philosophers has always contended. They have maintained that the tradition of theological and ethical knowledge is divinely preserved, and has a unity in itself; that there is a true traditive philosophy running down in the same channel with the divine tradition of faith, recognised by faith, known by the light of nature, and guarded by the circle of supernatural truths by which faith has surrounded it. In saying this, I am not extending the infallibility of the Church to philosophical or political questions apart from their contact with revelation; but affirming only that the radical truths of the natural order have become rooted in the substance of faith, and are guaranteed to us by the witness and custody of the Church. So likewise, as the laws of Christian civilisation are the laws of natural morality elevated by the Christian law, which is expounded and applied by the Church, there is a tradition both of private and public ethics—or, in other words, of morality and jurisprudence—which forms the basis of all personal duty, and of all political justice. In this, again, the Church has a discernment, and therefore a voice. A distribution of labour in the cultivation of all provinces of truth is prudent and intelligible. A division of authority and an exclusion of the Church from science is not only a dismemberment of the kingdom of truth, but a forcible rending of certain truths from their highest evidence. Witness the treatment of the question whether the existence of God can be proved and whether God can be known by natural reason in the hands of those who turn their backs upon the tradition of evidence in the universal Church. Unless revelation be an illusion, the voice of the Church must be heard in these higher provinces of human knowledge. "Newton," as Dr. Newman says, "cannot dispense with the metaphysician, nor the metaphysician with us." Into cosmogony the Church must enter by the doctrine of creation; into natural theology, by the doctrine of the existence and perfections of God; into ethics, by the doctrine of the cardinal virtues; into politics, by the indissolubility of marriage, the root of human society, as divorce is its dissolution. And by this interpenetration and interweaving of its teaching the Church binds all sciences to itself. They meet in it as in their proper centre. As the sovereign power which runs into all provinces unites them in one empire, so the voice and witness of the Church unites and binds all sciences in one.

'It is the parcelling and morselling out of science, and this disintegration of the tradition of truth, which has reduced the intellectual culture of England to its present fragmentary and contentious state. Not only errors are generated, but truths are set in opposition; science and revelation are supposed to be at variance, and revelation to be the weaker side of human knowledge.

'The Church has an infallible knowledge of the original revelation. Its definitions of Divine Faith fall within this limit; but its infallible judgments reach beyond it. The Church possesses a knowledge of truth which belongs also to the natural order. The existence of God—His power, goodness, and perfections—the moral law written in the conscience—are truths of the natural order which are declared also by revelation, and recorded in Holy Scripture. These truths the Church knows by a twofold light—by the supernatural light of revelation, and by the natural light which all men possess. In the Church this natural light is concentrated as in a focus. The great endowment of common sense—that is, the *communis sensus generis humani*, the maximum of light and evidence for certain truths of the natural order—resides eminently in the collective intelligence of the Church; that is to say, in the intelligence of the faithful, which is the seat of its passive infallibility, and in the intelligence of the pastors, or the *Magisterium Ecclesiæ*, which is the organ of its active infallibility. That two and two make four, is not more evident to the Catholic Church than to the rest of mankind, to S. Thomas or S. Bonaventura, than to Spinoza and Comte. But that God exists, and that man is responsible, because free, are moral truths, and for the perception of moral truths, even of the natural order, a moral discernment is needed; and the moral discernment of the Church, even of natural truths, is, I maintain, incomparably higher than the moral discernment of the mass of mankind, by virtue of its elevation to greater purity and conformity to the laws of nature itself.

'The highest object of human science is God; and theology, properly so called, is the science of His nature and perfections, the radiance which surrounds "the Father of lights, in whom is no change, neither shadow of vicissitude." Springing from this central science flow the sciences of the works of God, in nature and in grace; and under the former fall not only the physical sciences, but those which relate to man and action—as morals, politics, and history. Now, the revelation God has given us rests for its centre upon God Himself, but in its course describes a circumference within which many truths of the natural order relating both to the world and to man are included. These the Church knows, not only by natural light, but by Divine revelation, and declares by Divine assistance. But these primary truths of the natural order are axioms and principles of the sciences within which they properly fall; and these truths of philosophy belong also to the domain of faith. The same truths are the object of faith and of science; they are the links which couple these sciences to revelation. How, then, can these sciences be separated from their relation to revealed truth without a false procedure? No Catholic could so separate them, for these truths enter within the dogma of faith. No Christian who believes in Holy Scripture could do so, for they are included in Holy Writ. No mere philosopher could do so, for thereby he would discard and perhaps place himself in opposition and discord with the maximum of evidence which is attainable on these primary verities, and therefore with the common sense not only of Christendom, but of mankind. In this I am not advocating a mixture or confusion of religion and philosophy,—which, as Lord Bacon says in his work "De Augmentis Scientiarum," will undoubtedly make an heretical religion, and an imaginary and fabulous philosophy,—but affirming that certain primary truths of both physical and ethical philosophy are delivered to us by revelation, and that we cannot neglect them as our starting-points in such sciences without a false procedure and a palpable forfeiture of truth. Such verities are, for instance, the existence of God, the creation of the world, the freedom of the will, the moral office of the conscience, and the like. Lord Bacon says again, "There may be veins and lines, but not sections or separations," in the great continent of Truth. All truths alike are susceptible of scientific method, and all of a religious treatment. The father of modern philosophy, as men of our day call him, so severe and imperious in maintaining the distinct province and process of science, is not the less peremptory and absolute as to the unity of all truth and the vital relation of all true science to the Divine philosophy of revelation.'

We are as little dazzled by the intellectual development of the Anticatholic science as by the pretensions of modern democracy. We see both going to pieces before our eyes. And *ex parte intellectûs et ex parte voluntatis* we submit ourselves to the Church of God, the mother and mistress of Christian science and Christian society, as our only guide and only redemption from the aberrations which spring from the reason, and the confusions which spring from the will of man.

CHAPTER III.

THE RELATION OF THE HOLY GHOST TO THE LETTER OF SCRIPTURE.

The two divine truths which reign, and will reign for ever over the whole kingdom of faith and of theology, are the infallibility of the Church, and the inspiration of the Scripture; or, in other words, the relation of the Holy Spirit of God to the Word of God written and unwritten.

These two divine truths, when contemplated as doctrines—or rather these two divine facts, when contemplated in the supernatural order of grace—have had, like other dogmas, their successive periods of simple affirmation and simple belief—incipient controversy and partial analysis—and will probably have their formal contradiction, their last analysis, and their final scientific definition.

The history of the infallibility of the Church and of the inspiration of Holy Scripture will then be written like as the history of the Immaculate Conception, which has now been closed by the dogmatic Bull of Pius IX.

It is far from my thoughts to pretend to give here the history of so great and delicate a doctrine as Inspiration, but it may not be unseasonable to trace a slight outline of a subject which has now fixed upon itself an anxious attention in our country at this time. The Protestant Reformation staked its existence upon the Bible; and as Protestants have extensively denied or undermined its inspiration, no other subject can be so vital to their religion, or more opportune for us.

The Church of England has lately been thrown into much excitement, and public opinion has been not a little scandalised, by the appearance of works denying in great part the inspiration of Holy Scripture. And yet there is nothing new in the rise of such errors. Error has its periodic times. What is passing now, has returned in every century, almost in every generation. It is not new to the Catholic Church to have to combat with the depravers of Holy Writ; for there has been a line and succession of gainsayers who have denied the Divine veracity and authenticity, either in whole or in part, of the written Word of God. Even in the lifetime of S. John the Cerinthians rejected all the New Testament except the Gospel of S. Matthew and the Book of Acts. In the second century, the Carpocratians rejected the whole of the Old Testament; Marcion and Cerdon denounced it as the fabrication of an evil deity, and acknowledged only the Gospel of S. Luke and the Epistles to Timothy and Titus. In the third century the Archontici rejected the Old Testament; the Apellitæ, the Severiani, and the Eucharitæ rejected most of the Old Testament and of the New. In the fourth, the Alogi, the Gnostics, and the Manichæans rejected the greater part both of the Jewish and of the Christian Scriptures. Faustus the Manichæan, and others, against whom S. Ambrose and S. Augustine wrote in the fourth and fifth centuries, accused the Old Testament of immorality, contradiction, and intrinsic incredibility, as others have done since. The Apocryphi received only the Prophets and Apostles. In the eighth century, the Albanenses, Bajolenses, Concordenses—names known only to students—repeated the errors of Marcion. Herman Rissuich, in the fifteenth century, rejected the whole of Scripture as imperfect and useless: David Georgius revived this impiety in the sixteenth century. Luther and his followers rejected the Epistle of S. James, the Hebrews, the third of S. John, the second of S. Peter, and the Apocalypse.

The Libertini held all the Scriptures to be fables. The Ambrosians, claiming for themselves divine revelations, despised both the Old Testament and the New. This brings us to the seventeenth century, in which modern infidelity began to appear, and the Rationalistic criticism to arise. In the eighteenth and the present century there is no book of the Old or New Testament which has not been rejected by some among the Rationalistic or Neologian critics of Germany. The author to whom the modern errors on the subject of Inspiration may be ascribed is Spinoza. He first reduced to a complete statement all the objections which can be brought against it. He was the father of the sceptical criticism which in the seventeenth century inundated Holland and Germany, and found its way over into England. It is a remarkable fact that Schleiermacher, whose writings have extensively propagated the Rationalistic movement both in Germany and in England, sacrificed a lock of his hair as a token of pious veneration on the grave of Spinoza.[1] After Spinoza, Le Clerc, in 1685, published his letters entitled 'Sentimens de quelques Théologiens de Hollande,' which excited a great sensation, especially in England. They were a mere reflection of Spinoza.

[1] Lee *On Inspiration*, App. C. p. 450.

It is, therefore, no new thing in the history of the Church, nor, indeed, in the history of England since the Reformation. From the Deistical writers down to Thomas Paine, there has never wanted a succession of critics and objectors who have assailed the extrinsic or intrinsic authority of Holy Scripture.

So far it is no new thing. But in one aspect, indeed, it is altogether new. It is new to find this form of scepticism put forth by writers of eminence for dignity and personal excellence, and mental cultivation, in the Church of England; by men too, who still profess not only a faith in Christianity, but fidelity to the Anglican Church. Hitherto these forms of sceptical unbelief have worked outside the Church of England, and in hostility against it. Now they are within, and professing to be of it and to serve it. Unpalatable as the truth may be, it is certain that a Rationalistic school imported from Germany has established itself within the Church of England; that its writers are highly respectable and cultivated men, and that though they may be few, yet the influence of their opinions is already widely spread, and that a very general sympathy with them already extends itself among the laity of the Anglican Church. This is certainly a phenomenon altogether new.

Before entering upon the subject of this chapter, it would seem, therefore, to be seasonable to examine briefly the present state of the subject of Inspiration in the Church of England, and contrast with it the teaching of the Catholic Church upon this point.

And first, as to the doctrine of the Church of England on Inspiration, it is to be remembered that though the Canon of Scripture was altered by the Anglican Reformation, the subject of Inspiration was hardly discussed. The traditional teaching of the Catholic Theology, with its various opinions, was therefore passively retained. The earlier writers, such as Hooker, repeat the traditional formulas respecting the inspiration and veracity of Holy Scripture. Hooker's words are, 'He (that is, God) so employed them (the Prophets) in this heavenly work, that they neither spake nor wrote a word of their own, but uttered syllable by syllable as the Spirit put it into their mouths.'[1] Such was more or less the tone of the chief Anglican writers for a century after the Reformation.

Perhaps the best example of the Anglican teaching on the subject will be found in Whitby's general Preface to his 'Paraphrase of the Gospels.' His opinion is as follows. He begins by adopting the

[1] *Works*, vol. iii. p. 62. Ed. Keble.

distinction of the Jewish Church between the 'Prophets' and the 'Chetubin,' or holy writers, and therefore between the 'inspiration of suggestion' and the 'inspiration of direction.'

He then lays down—

1. First, that where there was no antecedent knowledge of the matter to be written, an inspiration of suggestion was vouchsafed to the Apostles; but that where such knowledge did antecedently exist, there was only an inspiration exciting them to write such matters, and directing them in the writing so as to preclude all error.

2. Secondly, that in writing those things which were not antecedently known to them, either by natural reason including education, or previous revelation—*e.g.* the Incarnation, the vocation of the Gentiles, the apostacy of the latter times, the prophecies of the Apocalypse,—they had an immediate suggestion of the Holy Spirit.

3. Thirdly, that in all other matters they were directed so as to preclude error, and to confirm the truth whether by illumination in the meaning of the previous revelation, or by reasoning.

4. Fourthly, that in the historical parts of the New Testament they were directed in all that is necessary to the truth of the facts related, but not as to the

order or accessories of such events, unless these things affected the truth of the facts.

5. Fifthly, that in relating the words or discourses of our Lord and of others, they were directed so as to preclude all error as to the substance, but not so as to reproduce the words.

6. Lastly, that the inspiration or divine assistance of the sacred writers was such as 'will assure us of the truth of what they write, whether by inspiration of suggestion, or direction only; but not such as would imply that their very words were dictated, or their phrases suggested to them, by the Holy Ghost.'[1]

In Bishop Burnet may be seen a somewhat less explicit tone. He says, 'The laying down a scheme that asserts an immediate inspiration, which goes to the style, and to every tittle, and that denies any error to have crept *into any of the copies*, as it seems on the one hand to raise the honour of Scripture very highly, so it lies open on the other hand to great difficulties, which seem insuperable on that hypothesis.'[2]

Such was the current teaching of the most respectable class of Anglican divines, men of true learning

---

[1] Whitby's *Paraphrase*, Gen. Pref. pp. 5–7. Ed. London, 1844.
[2] Burnet, *Exposition of the Thirty-nine Articles*, p. 117. Ed. Oxford.

and of sound judgment, in the best century of the Church of England. But I need quote no more. Let us now examine one or two of the modern opinions on the same subject.

A member of the University of Oxford writes as follows:—'The Bible is none other than the voice of Him that sitteth upon the throne. Every book of it, every chapter of it, every verse of it, every word of it, every syllable of it, every letter of it, is the direct utterance of the Most High.'[1] A member of Trinity College, Dublin, writes as follows;—'The opinion that the subject-matter alone of the Bible proceeded from the Holy Spirit, while its language was left to the unaided choice of the various writers, amounts to that fantastic notion which is the grand fallacy of many theories of Inspiration; namely, that two different spiritual agencies were in operation, one of which produced the phraseology in its outward form, while the other created within the soul the conceptions and thoughts of which such phraseology was the expression. The Holy Spirit, on the contrary, as the productive *principle*, embraces the entire activity of those whom He inspires, rendering their language the Word of God. The entire substance

---

[1] Burgon, *Inspiration and Interpretation of Holy Scripture*, p. 89, quoted by Dr. Colenso, part 1. p. 6.

and form of Scripture, whether resulting from revelation or natural knowledge, are thus blended together into one harmonious whole.'[1] Once more. Dr. Arnold writes as follows:—'An inspired work is supposed to mean a work to which God has communicated His own perfections; so that the slightest error or defect of any kind in it is inconceivable, and that which is other than perfect in all points cannot be inspired. This is the unwarrantable interpretation of the word Inspiration. . . . Surely many of our words and many of our actions are spoken and done by the inspiration of God's Spirit. . . . Yet does the Holy Spirit so inspire us as to communicate to us His own perfections? Are our best works or words utterly free from error or from sin?'[2] Mr. Jowett, in his well-known Essay on the 'Interpretation of Scripture,' after reciting the commonly-received theories of Inspiration, proceeds as follows:—'Nor for any of the higher or supernatural views of Inspiration is there any foundation in the Gospels or Epistles. There is no appearance in their writings that the Evangelists or Apostles had any inward gift, or were subject to any power external to them different from that of preaching or

---

[1] Lee *On the Inspiration of Holy Scripture*, pp. 32, 33.
[2] Arnold's *Sermons*, quoted by Stanley, *The Bible, its Form, and its Substance*, Preface, vii. viii. ix.

teaching which they daily exercised; nor do they anywhere lead us to suppose that they were free from error or infirmity. . . . The nature of Inspiration can only be known from the examination of Scripture. There is no other source to which we can turn for information; and we have no right to assume some imaginary doctrine of Inspiration like the infallibility of the Roman Catholic Church. To the question What is Inspiration? the first answer therefore is, That idea of Scripture which we gather from the knowledge of it.'[1] Dr Williams says, 'In the Bible, as an expression of devout reason, and therefore to be read with reason in freedom, he [Bunsen] finds a record of the spiritual giants whose experience generated the religious atmosphere we breathe.'

I do not undertake to do more than recite these opinions of clergymen of the Church of England. It is not for us to say what is the authoritative doctrine of that body; but it has been recently declared by the highest Ecclesiastical tribunal, that the views of inspiration last given are not inconsistent with the Anglican formularies. Dr. Lushington expressed himself as follows:—'As to the liberty of the Anglican clergy to examine and determine the text of Scrip-

[1] *Essays and Reviews*, pp. 345, 347.

ture, I exceedingly ... doubt if this liberty can be extended beyond the limits I have mentioned, namely, certain verses or parts of Scripture. I think it could not be permitted to a clergyman to reject the whole of one of the books of Scripture.'[1]

It is evident from the above quotations that the theory of Inspiration among many prominent men in the Anglican Church has been moving in the direction of the German Neology.

Let us now turn to the Catholic doctrine. The Catholic Church has expressed itself authoritatively on the subject of Holy Scripture and its Divine character in the following points:—

1. That the writings of the Prophets and Apostles are Holy Scripture; or in other words, that certain sacred books exist in its custody in which the 'veritas et disciplina' of Christ is partly contained; 'perspiciens hanc veritatem et disciplinam contineri in libris scriptis et sine scripto traditionibus.'[2]

2. That God is the Author of these sacred books. It declares both the books and the traditions to be given to the Church, 'Spiritu Sancto dictante,' by God Himself, and that He is the Author of all such books and traditions, both of the Old and of the

---

[1] Judgment—Bishop of Salisbury *versus* Williams, p. 16.
[2] *Concil. Trid.* sess. iv.

New Testament: 'omnes libros tam Veteris quam Novi Testamenti, quum utriusque unus Deus sit auctor.'[1]

3. That the sacred books are so many in number, and are such by name; that is, the catalogue or canon of the Old and New Testament. The canon declared by the Council of Trent is that of the Council of Florence in the fourteenth century, of Constantinople in the sixth, of Carthage in the fourth, and of the Pontifical declarations of S. Innocent and S. Gelasius.

4. That these books in their integrity, and with all their parts 'libros integros cum omnibus suis partibus,' are to be held as sacred and canonical; that is, to be inspired, and to have God for their Author, which excludes the supposition that any part of such books is merely of human authorship, and therefore that falsehood or error can be found in them. This declaration, though made explicitly of the Latin version called the Vulgate, applies à fortiori to the Holy Scriptures objectivè sumptæ. It is made also under anathema.

5. That the Latin version called the Vulgate is authentic, 'pro authentica habeatur.'[2]

These five points are, I believe, all that the Catholic Church has authoritatively declared. To

---

[1] *Concil. Trid.* sess. iv.   [2] Ibid.

these every Catholic yields assent. But beyond these nothing is of obligation. And whatsoever I may add belongs to the region, not of faith, but of theology, not of the Councils and Pontiffs, but of the Schools.

And first we will begin with the period of simple faith.

The Catholic Church, in inheriting the canon of the Hebrew and of the Hellenistic books from the synagogue, inherited with them the belief of inspiration current among the Jews, by whom the operations of the Divine Spirit were believed to extend to the whole substance and form, the sense and the letter, of Holy Scripture.

Such was evidently the belief of the early Christian writers. The writings of the Fathers both of the East and West show that they extended the inspiration of the Holy Ghost to the whole of Scripture, both to its substance and to its form; so that it is altogether pervaded by the mind, voice, and authority of God.

For instance, S. Irenæus says, 'The Scriptures are perfect, being dictated by the Word of God and by His Spirit.'[1]

---

[1] 'Scripturæ quidem perfectæ sunt, quippe a Verbo Dei et Spiritu ejus dictæ.'—S. Iren. *Cont. Hær.* lib. ii. cap. 28, al. 47.

S. Macarius says, 'God the King sent the Holy Scriptures as His epistles to men.'[1]

S. John Chrysostom says, 'What things the Scriptures promulgate, the Lord promulgated.'[2] Again, 'All that is in Scripture we must thoroughly examine; for all are dictated by the Holy Ghost, and nothing is written in them in vain.'[3] Again, 'The mouth of the Prophet is the mouth of God.'[4] Again, 'The Divine Scripture declares nothing vaguely or without intention, but every syllable and every point has some mystery hidden in it.'[5] Not an iota, not a point, in Scripture is there in vain.[6] Again, 'Nothing in the Divine Scriptures is superfluous, for they are dictated by the Holy Ghost.' These might

---

[1] Τὰς θείας γραφὰς ὥσπερ ἐπιστολὰς ἀπέστολεν ὁ βασιλεὺς θεὸς τοῖς ἀνθρώποις. S. Macar. *Hom. xxxix.* p. 476.

[2] Ἃ δὲ αἱ γραφαὶ φθέγγονται, ταῦτα ὁ δεσπότης ἐφθέγξατο. S. Chrys. *De Lazaro, Concio* iv. tom. i. p. 755.

[3] Οὕτω καὶ ἐν ταῖς θείαις γραφαῖς, ἰῶτα ἓν ἢ μίαν κεραίαν οὐκ ἀζήμιον παραδραμεῖν, ἀλλὰ πάντα διερευνᾶσθαι χρή· πνεύματι γὰρ ἁγίῳ πάντα εἴρηται, καὶ οὐδὲν παρέλκον ἐν αὐταῖς. *Hom. xxxvi. in Joan.* tom. viii. p. 206.

[4] Οὕτω καὶ τὸ στόμα τῶν προφητῶν, στόμα ἐστι τοῦ θεοῦ. *Hom. xiv. in Acta Apost.* tom. ix. p. 159.

[5] Οὐδὲν γὰρ ἁπλῶς καὶ ὡς ἔτυχεν φθέγγεται ἡ θεία γραφή, ἀλλὰ κἂν συλλαβὴ τυγχάνῃ, κἂν κεραία μία, ἔχει τινὰ ἐγκεκρυμμένον θησαυρόν. *Hom. xviii. in Gen.* tom. iv. p. 156.

[6] Οὐδὲ γὰρ συλλαβὴ, οὐδὲ κεραία μία ἐστὶν ἐγκειμένη παρὰ τῇ γραφῇ, ᾗ μὴ πολὺς ἐναπόκειται θησαυρὸς ἐν τῷ βάθει. *Hom. xxi. in Gen.* tom. iv. p. 180.

be extended to any length. S. Basil says, 'Let therefore the Scriptures, which are inspired of God, decide for us.'[1] S. Gregory of Nazianzum says, 'But we who extend the diligence (*i.e.* the operation) of the Spirit even to every, the least point and line (of the Scriptures) will never grant, for it is not right we should, that even the least actions by them commemorated were written without intention.'[2] S. Gregory Nyssen says, 'Whatever the Sacred Scriptures declare are the utterances of the Holy Ghost. Therefore, the holy Prophets filled by God are inspired by the power of the Holy Ghost, and the whole of Scripture is therefore said to be divinely inspired.'[3] I will only add one more. S. John Damascene says, 'The Law, Prophets, Evangelists and Apostles, Pastors and Doctors, spoke by the Holy Ghost; so that the whole Scripture inspired by God without doubt is useful.'[4]

[1] Ἡ θεόπνευστος ἡμῖν διαιτησάτω γραφή. S. Basilius, *Ep.* 189, ad *Eustath.* tom. iii. p. 277.

[2] Ἡμεῖς δὲ οἱ καὶ μέχρι τῆς τυχούσης κεραίας καὶ γραμμῆς τοῦ πνεύματος τὴν ἀκρίβειαν ἕλκοντες, οὔ ποτε δεξόμεθα, οὐ γὰρ ὅσιον, οὐδὲ τὰς ἐλαχίστας πράξεις εἰκῆ σπουδασθῆναι τοῖς ἀναγράψασι, καὶ μέχρι τοῦ παρόντος μνήμῃ διασωθῆναι. S. Greg. Nazian. *Orat. ii.* tom. i. p. 60.

[3] Ὅσα ἡ θεία γραφὴ λέγει, τοῦ πνεύματος εἰσι τοῦ ἁγίου φωναί. . . . καὶ διὰ τοῦτο πᾶσα γραφὴ θεόπνευστος λέγεται, διὰ τὸ τῆς θείας ἐμπνεύσεως εἶναι διδασκαλίαν. S. Greg. Nyss. *Orat. vi. cont. Eunom.* tom. ii. p. 605.

[4] Διὰ πνεύματος τοίνυν ἁγίου, ὅτε νόμος καὶ οἱ προφῆται, εὐαγγελισ-

For the Latin Fathers, passages might be indefinitely multiplied. The following will suffice. S. Augustine says of the Scripture, 'In it God Himself speaks.'[1] 'Holy Scripture is the handwriting of God,'[2] 'the adorable style and pen of the Spirit of God.'[3] 'The faith wavers if the authority of the Divine Scriptures is shaken.'[4] 'They are labouring to destroy the authority of the Holy Scripture, who ascribe to it any falsehood.'[5]

S. Gregory the Great says, 'The Author of the book is the Holy Ghost. He therefore wrote these things who dictated them to be written. He Himself wrote who inspired them in the act of writing.[6]

ται καὶ ἀπόστολοι, καὶ ποιμένες ἐλάλησαν καὶ διδάσκαλοι. πᾶσα τοίνυν γραφὴ θεόπνευστος, πάντως καὶ ὠφέλιμος. S. Joan. Damas. *De Fid. Orth.* lib. iv. cap. 17.

[1] 'O homo, nempe quod Scriptura mea dicit, ego dico.'—S. Aug. *Confess.* lib. xiii. cap. 44, tom. i. p. 241.

[2] 'Scriptura Dei manere debet, et quoddam chirographum Dei, quod omnes transeuntes legerent.'—*Enarrat. in Psal. calix.* cap. 17, tom. i. p. 1620.

[3] 'Avidissime arripui venerabilem stilum Spiritus tui.'—*Confess.* vii. 27, tom. i. p. 143.

[4] 'Titubabit autem fides, si divinarum Scripturarum vacillat auctoritas.'—*De Doct. Christ.* i. 41, tom. iii. p. 18.

[5] 'Ut dicant hoc auctorem libri non verum dixisse. . . . Scripturae sanctae auctoritatem frangere conantur.'—*De Sanct. Virg.* cap. 17, tom. vi. p. 348.

[6] 'Auctor libri Spiritus Sanctus fideliter credatur. Ipse igitur haec scripsit, qui scribenda dictavit. Ipse scripsit qui et in illius opere inspirator extitit, et per scribentis vocem imitanda ad nos ejus facta transmisit.'—S. Greg. *Moral. in Job. praef.* i. 2, tom. i. p. 7.

Whatsoever the Fathers declare in the sacred oracles, they declare not from themselves, but they received them from God.'[1]

S. Ambrose, speaking of the sacred authors, says, 'They wrote not by art, but by grace. For they wrote those things which the Spirit gave them to speak.'[2]

Such are the statements of three of the four great Doctors of the Church.

It is clear that these Fathers had no thought of error or uncertainty in the sacred text, but extended the dictation of the Holy Spirit to the whole extent of the books of the Old and New Testament as simply the Word of God. They may be taken to represent the mind of the whole Church in the ages which went before the period of controversy as to the nature of Inspiration.

The next period of the subject is that of analysis as to the nature and limits of Inspiration. But as I am not pretending to write its history, all I will attempt is to state the two opinions which exist

---

[1] 'Patres quidquid per sacra eloquia loquuntur non a semetipsis sed a Domino acceperunt.'—*III. in prim. Reg.* i. 8, tom. iii. pars 2, p. 115.

[2] 'Non secundum artem scripserunt, sed secundum gratiam, quæ super omnem artem est; scripserunt enim quæ Spiritus iis loqui dabat.'—S. Amb. *Ep. viii.* 1, tom. iii. p. 817.

among Catholic theologians since the Council of Trent.

1. The first is that of the older writers, who maintain that every particle and word of the Canonical books was written by the dictation of the Holy Spirit.

Such, as I have shown, was certainly the language—I will not say the opinion—of most of the Fathers both of the East and of the West. They spoke of the New Testament much as the Elder Church spoke of the Old. I say the language—not the opinion—because it is evident that they were occupied with the sole intention of affirming the Canonical books to be the Word of God, without entering analytically into the questions which a later criticism forced upon the Scholastic theologians.

This opinion is stated by Habert in the Prolegomena to his Theology as follows: 'Tostatus on Numbers, chap. xi., Estius on 2 Timothy, chap. iii.,[1] and many theologians of weight, affirm that every word was inspired and dictated by the Holy Spirit, so that the composition and style of the language is to be ascribed to Him. The Faculties of Louvain

---

[1] 'Recte igitur et verissime ex hoc loco statuitur omnem Scripturam sacram et canonicam Spiritu Sancto dictante esse conscriptam; ita nimirum ut non solum sententiæ sed et verba singula et verborum ordo, ac tota dispositio sit a Deo tanquam per semetipsum loquente aut scribente.'—Estius, *Comm. in. II. Tim. iii.*, 16, tom. ii. p. 826.

and Douai censure the opposite opinion as a departure from orthodoxy. So in their censure they declare, 'It is an intolerable and great blasphemy, if any shall affirm that any otiose word can be found in Scripture. All the words of Scripture are so many sacraments (or mysteries). Every phrase, syllable, tittle, and point is full of a divine sense, as Christ says in S. Matthew, "a jot or a tittle shall not pass from the law."'[1] They go on to quote S. John Chrysostom, S. Augustine, S. Bernard, and the Fathers generally.

Melchior Canus is supposed to be of this opinion.[2] In his second book *De Locis Theol.*, after stating and refuting the opinions 'of those who thought that the sacred writers in the Canonical books did not always speak by the Divine Spirit,' he esta-

---

[1] '*Q. 3. Singula Scripturæ verba suntne a Spiritu Sancto inspirata et dictata, ita ut vocabulorum compositio et stylus ad ipsum referenda sint?*

'*R.* Duplex est in Scholis opposita sententia; Tostatus in cap. xi. Num., Estius in cap. iii. II. ad Tim., et plures graves Theologi illud affirmant, imò Lovanienses et Duacenses sententiam oppositam notant, ut minùs orthodoxam, sic enim inquiunt in suis censuris; *Intoleranda prorsus et grandis blasphemia est; si quis vel verbum asserat in Scripturis inveniri otiosum.* . . . *Singula verba Scripturarum singula sunt Sacramenta, singuli sermones, syllabæ, apices, puncta divinis plena sunt sensibus,* ait enim Christus Matth. v. *jota unum, aut unus apex non prætcribit a lege.* . . .'—Habert, *Theol. Dogmat. et Moral. Proleg.*, tom. i. pp. 41, 42.

[2] Melchior Canus, *Loc. Theol.* lib. ii. cap. xvii.

blishes the following proposition: that 'every particle of the Canonical books was written by the assistance of the Holy Spirit.' He says, 'I admit that the sacred writers had no need of a proper and express revelation in writing every particle of the Scripture; but that every part of the Scripture was written by a peculiar instinct and impulse of the Holy Ghost, I truly and rightly contend.' After saying that some things were known to them by supernatural revelation, and others by natural knowledge, he adds, 'that they did not need a supernatural light and express revelation to write these latter truths, but they needed the presence and peculiar help of the Holy Ghost, that these things, though they were human truths, and known by natural reason, should nevertheless be written divinely and without any error.'

The same is also the teaching of Bañez, and of the Dominican theologians generally.

2. The other opinion, which is that of Bellarmine, —and I believe I may say, of the Jesuit theologians, and of a majority of the more recent writers on Inspiration,—is, that the whole *matter* of Holy Scripture was written by the assistance of the Holy Spirit, but not the whole *form* dictated by Him; or, in other words, 'res et sententias'—the sense

and substance; 'non verba et apices'—not every particular word or letter.

But, before we enter into the detail of this question, it may be well to give, in a few words, the history of a controversy which, in the sixteenth and seventeenth centuries, promoted the analysis of the subject, and left it in its present form. It may be said to have arisen out of the excesses of the Lutheran Reformation.

The account given by Mosheim of the opinions of Luther and of the Lutherans is as follows. He says that Luther taught that the *matter* of the Holy Scripture—that is, the truths contained in it—are from the Holy Ghost; but the *form*—that is, the style, words, phrases, and construction—are from the writer. When Catholic theologians replied that this opened the way for error into the sacred text, certain followers of Luther went into the other extreme, and taught, as the younger Buxtorf,[1] that the Hebrew vowel-points and accents are inspired.

It appears also that Erasmus expressed himself at one time with very little caution. In his Commentary on the 2nd chapter of S. Matthew, he said, 'Sive quod ipsi Evangelistæ testimonia hujusmodi non e libris deprompserunt; sed memoriæ fidentes

[1] Lee *On Inspiration*, Appendix C. p. 436.

ita ut lapsi sint.' 'Whether it be that the Evangelists did not draw their narratives from records, but trusted to their memory, and so fell into error.' Eckius wrote to him, 'Audi, mi Erasme, arbitrarisne Christianum patienter laturum Evangelistas in Evangeliis lapsos? Si hic vacillat S. Scripturæ auctoritas, quæ pars alia sine suspicione erit?'[1] Erasmus was attacked by the Salmanticenses and other Spanish theologians. He afterwards explains himself, though not very firmly or frankly, but the objectionable words were erased from the next edition of his Commentary.

The next discussion on the subject of Inspiration, among Catholic theologians, arose during the Jansenist Controversy. In 1586, Lessius and Hamel, in their lectures at Louvain, taught the following propositions:—

1. 'Ut aliquid sit Scriptura Sacra, non est necessarium, singula ejus verba inspirata esse a Spiritu Sancto.' 'That a book be Holy Scripture, it is not necessary that every word of it be inspired by the Holy Ghost.'

2. 'Non est necessarium ut singulæ veritates et sententiæ sint immediate a Spiritu Sancto ipsi scrip-

---

[1] Lee *On Inspiration*, Appendix C. p. 437. *Erasmi Opp.* ep, 303, tom. iii. 296.

tori inspiratæ.' 'It is not necessary that every truth or sentence be immediately inspired into the writer by the Holy Ghost.'

3. 'Liber aliquis (qualis forte est secundus Machabæorum) humana industria sine assistentia Spiritus Sancti scriptus, si Spiritus Sanctus postea testetur nihil ibi esse falsum, efficitur Scriptura Sacra.'[1] 'A book (such as perhaps the 2nd of Maccabees), written by human industry, without the assistance of the Holy Ghost—if the Holy Spirit afterwards testify that nothing false is contained in it—becomes Holy Scripture.'

These propositions were at once assailed. The Archbishops of Cambrai and Mechlin sent them to the Faculties of Douai and Louvain.[2] They were condemned by both. The third was especially censured. Estius, who drew up the censure, in his 'Commentary on the Epistles' gives his own opinion as follows: 'From this passage it is rightly and truly established, that all the sacred and canonical Scripture is written by the dictation of the Holy Ghost; so that not only the sense, but every word, and the order of the words, and the whole arrangement, is from God, as if He were speaking or writing in person. For this is

---

[1] See *Theol. Wirceburg.* tom. i. p. 23.
[2] See *Theol. Wirceburg.* tom. i. p. 23.

the meaning of the Scripture being divinely inspired.'[1]

Lessius and Hamel appealed to the Sorbonne. The Faculty of Paris did not approve either of the Jesuit propositions, nor of the censures of Louvain and Douai. The Faculties of Mayence, Treves, Ingoldstadt, and Rome disapproved the censures; but Sixtus V. imposed silence until the Holy See should pronounce. The subject has never been decided. The censures are given by D'Argentre, in his 'Collectio Judiciorum de novis Erroribus,' and the Jesuit propositions are defended by P. Simon, in his 'Histoire Critique du Texte du Nouveau Testament.'[2]

About fifty years after, that is in A.D. 1650, Holden published his 'Divinæ Fidei Analysis,' in which he maintained a theory of inspiration which is certainly open to some, if not to all the censures which were directed against it. I hope, however, that his orthodoxy may be maintained, though somewhat at the expense of his coherence.

The passage which caused the censure of P. Simon is to be found in the fifth chapter of the first book, and is as follows:—' Auxilium speciale divinum præstitum auctori cujuslibet scripti, quod pro verbo Dei

---

[1] *Estii Comment. in Ep.* 2 *ad Timoth.* cap. iii. 16.
[2] Simon, *Histoire*, &c., ch. xxiii.

recipit Ecclesia, ad ea solummodo se porrigit, quæ vel sint pure doctrinalia, vel proximum aliquem, aut necessarium habeant ad doctrinalia respectum : in iis vero quæ non sunt de instituto Scriptoris vel ad alia referuntur, eo tantum subsidio Deum illi adfuisse judicamus, quod piissimis cæteris auctoribus commune sit.'[1]

This, at first sight at least, would seem to imply that in all matters not of faith or morals the inspired writers were liable to err like any other pious men. Nevertheless, in three places Holden affirms that the books of Scripture are absolutely free from all error. In the first section of the same chapter he defines the Scripture as a document containing truth, and nothing 'a veritate quacunque dissonam vel alienam.' In the third he says, 'Quamvis enim nullam complectatur Scriptura falsitatem.' In the third chapter of the second book he says, 'Quamvis falsitatis arguere non licet quicquid habetur in Sacro Codice, veruntamen quæ ad religionem non spectant, Catholicæ Fidei articulos nullatenus astruunt.' It is evident, then, that he denied the presence of anything false or erroneous in Holy Scripture; that if he limited the infallible assistance of the Holy Spirit to matters of faith and morals, he supposed that the whole of the sacred text was written by such assistance

[1] *Divinæ Fidei Analysis*, lib. i. c. v. p. 48.

as, in fact, excluded all error; or, in other words, that if the sacred writers in other matters might have erred, they never did.

I notice this because it is well to show how little the name of Holden may be quoted by those who, at this day, maintain that the inspired writers, in matters not of faith and morals, did err; and because even the writer in Bergier's Dictionary seems so to represent him, and, I regret to add, Père Matignon.[1]

We have now before us the main lines of opinion which have existed among Catholic divines on the subject of Inspiration. They have never been much modified to this day. The one affirms the inspiration both of the matter and the form of Holy Scripture; the other, of the matter only, except so far as the doctrine of faith and morals, all error of every kind being excluded by a special and infallible assistance. To these two opinions some would add that of Holden as a third; namely, that this special assistance is limited to faith and morals, all error being nevertheless excluded, though the assistance in other subject-matters is only of an ordinary kind; but, I think, without sufficient foundation, for the reasons I have given.

In order to appreciate more exactly the reach of

[1] *La Liberté de l'esprit humain dans la Foi Catholique*, p. 187.

these opinions, it will be well to examine them somewhat more intimately, and to fix the sense of the terms used in the discussion of the subject.

(1) First, then, comes the word *Inspiration*, which is often confounded with *Revelation*.

Inspiration, in its *first intention*, signifies the action of the Divine Spirit upon the human, that is, upon the intelligence and upon the will. It is an intelligent and vital action of God upon the soul of man; and 'inspired' is to be predicated, not of books or truths, but of living agents.

In its *second intention*, it signifies the action of the Spirit of God upon the intelligence and will of man, whereby any one is impelled and enabled to act, or to speak, or to write, in some special way designed by the Spirit of God.

In its still more *special* and *technical intention*, it signifies an action of the Spirit upon men, impelling them to write what God reveals, suggests, or wills that they should write. But inspiration does not necessarily signify revelation, or suggestion of the matter to be written.

(2) Secondly, *Revelation* signifies the unfolding to the intelligence of man truths which are contained in the intelligence of God, the knowledge of which without such revelation would be impossible. Men

may be the subjects of revelation, and not of inspiration; and they might be the subjects of inspiration, and not of revelation.

(3) Thirdly, *Suggestion*, in the theory of inspiration, signifies the bringing to mind such things as God wills the writer to put in writing. All revelation is suggestion, but not all suggestion revelation; because much that is suggested may be of the natural order, needing no revelation, being already known by natural reason, or by historical tradition and the like.

(4) Fourthly, by *Assistance* is understood the presence and help of the Holy Spirit, by which the human agent, in full use of his own liberty and powers—such as natural gifts, genius, acquired cultivation, and the like,—executes the work which the Divine Inspiration impels him to write.

There are three kinds of *assistance*.

(1) First, there is the assistance afforded by the Holy Spirit to all the faithful, by which their intelligence is illuminated and their will strengthened, without exempting them from the liability to error.

(2) Secondly, there is the assistance vouchsafed to the Church diffused throughout the world or congregated in council, or to the person of the Vicar of Jesus Christ, speaking *ex cathedrâ*, which excludes all liability to error within the sphere of faith and

morals, and such facts and truths as attach to them (of which relations the Church is the ultimate judge), but does not extend to the other orders of purely natural science and knowledge.

(3) Lastly, there is the assistance granted as a 'gratia gratis data' to the inspired writers of the Holy Scripture, which excludes all liability to error in the act of writing, not only in matters of faith and morals, but in all matters, of whatsoever kind, which by the inspiration of God they are impelled to write.

The Jesuits, in the 'Theologia Wirceburgensis,' sum up the subject in the following way:—The authorship of God 'may be conceived in three ways. First, *by special assistance*, which preserves the writer from all error and falsehood. Secondly, *by inspiration*, which impels the writer to the act of writing, without, however, destroying his liberty. Thirdly, *by revelation*, by which truths hitherto unknown are manifested.' They then affirm, 'that God specially inspired the sacred writers with the truths and matter expressed in the sacred books.'[1]

---

[1] 'Triplex concipi potest modus, quo Deus mentem scriptoris alicujus afficiat. 1ᵘˢ est *specialis assistentia*, stans in peculiari auxilio, quo Deus ita adest scriptori, ut ne inter scribendum erret aut mentiendo, aut falsum proferendo, aut defectum quemcumque committendo, qui impediat, ne scriptio ad Dei directionem referri queat: 2ᵘˢ est *inspiratio*, quæ præter specialem assistentiam dicit

Perhaps it may be more in accordance with the facts of the case to invert the order, and to say that what we call Inspiration, in the special and technical sense, includes the three following operations of the Holy Ghost upon the mind of the sacred writers :—

(1) First, the impulse to put in writing the matter which God wills they should record.

(2) Secondly, the suggestion of the matter to be written, whether by revelation of truths not previously known, or only by the prompting of those things which were already within the writer's knowledge.

(3) Thirdly, the assistance which excludes liability to error in writing all things, whatsoever may be suggested to them by the Spirit of God to be written.

From this follow two corollaries :—

1. That in Holy Scripture there can be no falsehood or error.

2. That God is the author of all inspired books.

The enunciation of those two axioms of Christianity has elicited in all ages a series of objections. It

incitationem quamdam interiorem motumque insolitum, quo quis ad scribondum impellitur, sine rationis tamen et libertatis periculo : 3ᵘᵃ est *revelatio*, quæ memoratæ inspirationi superaddit veritatis antea ignotæ factam divinitus manifestationem.

'*Dico I.*°—Deus res saltem seu veritates et sententias in libris sacris expressas Scriptoribus sacris specialiter inspiravit.'—*Theol. Wirceburg.* tom. i. pp. 15, 16.

would be impossible to enumerate or to recite them all: I will, therefore, take only the chief categories, so to say, of the difficulties which are supposed to exist in Holy Scripture.

1. First, it was alleged by the Manichæans or Marcionites that the Old Testament was both evil and discordant with the New. S. Augustine wrote a book called 'Contra Adversarium Legis et Prophetarum,' in refutation of a manuscript said to be found at Carthage in a street by the sea-shore, and read in public to the people, 'multis confluentibus, et adtentissime audientibus.' The sum of the book was, that the maker of the world was evil, and the creator of evil; that he was cruel, because he inflicted death for trifling causes, as on the sons of Heli, also upon infants and innocents; that he could not be the true God, because he delighted in sacrifices: and that the Flood was not sent because of sin, because mankind was worse after it than before.[1] I need not give more examples: I quote these only to show that this form of objection is not new.

2. Secondly, it has been objected that the Evangelists are discordant with each other. This also was treated by S. Augustine, by S. John Chrysostom, and has produced a whole Bibliotheca of Harmonies.

[1] S. Aug. tom. viii. p. 550.

3. Thirdly, that the Holy Scriptures contain errors in science, history, chronology, and the like.

This objection is chiefly of modern date. The late Dr. Arnold expresses himself as follows:—' I would not give unnecessary pain to any one by an enumeration of those points in which the literal historical statement of an inspired writer has been vainly defended. Some instances will probably occur to most readers; others are, perhaps, not known, and never will be known to many.'[1] His disciples naturally follow the same line. The writers of the 'Essays and Reviews' are bolder and more explicit.

It is, however, with surprise that I find the Abbé Le Noir writing in these terms: 'There are in Holy Scripture faults of geography, chronology, natural history, of physical science—of science generally: in short, perhaps, also philosophical inaccuracies and literary errors against real and unchangeable good taste.' These faults, he says, concern 'the idea itself,' that is, the *matter* of Holy Scripture, not the *form* only, ' and are not to be explained by errors of copyists.'[2]

4. Fourthly, that the Holy Scripture contains expressions of hope, uncertainty, and of intentions

---

[1] Dr. Stanley *On the Bible*, &c., Preface, p. ix.
[2] *Dictionnaire des Harmonies de la Raison et de la Foi*, pp. 921, 2.

never accomplished; of advice declared to be simply personal, not of Divine suggestion; all of which are evidently of human authorship, and therefore liable to error.[1]

---

[1] In order to show that the inspired writers did not always write by inspiration, and that what they wrote without inspiration they wrote only as men liable to error, a well-known writer has lately quoted such passages as the following from the commentaries of S. Jerome on the words of S. Paul: 'Although I be rude in speech, yet not in knowledge' (2 Cor. xi. 6).

'Therefore Hebrew of the Hebrews as he was, and most learned in his vernacular tongue, he was not able to express the profundity of his meaning in a language not his own: nor did he much heed the words so long as the sense was secure' (S. Hieron. Com. lib. iii. ad Gal. cap. vi. tom. iv. p. 309).

Again, on the third chapter to the Ephesians he says: 'He, therefore, who committed solecisms in his words, and could not express an hyperbole or complete a sentence, boldly claims for himself wisdom, and says, according to the revelation the mystery is made known unto me' (Ib. ad Ephes. cap. vi. lib. ii. p. 348).

Once more, in the Epistle to Algasia on the words, 'Although I be rude in speech, yet not in knowledge,' he says: 'Paul said this not out of humility but in truth of conscience.' . . . 'He does not fully express his profound and recondite meaning by his speech, and though he himself knew what he said, I conceive that he was not able to transfer it in speech to the ears of others' (Ib. tom. iv. p. 204). These passages might be easily multiplied, and others also, where he speaks as a man carried away by human infirmity (ad Gal. cap. v. ib. p. 293).

These passages not only fall short of the conclusion for which they are quoted, but overturn it. For S. Paul expressly affirms that though he was rude in speech he was not in knowledge, which S. Jerome interprets to be his consciousness of 'profound and recondite meanings,' and also of wisdom. But this excludes the supposition of all error. For solecisms in words and the limitations of a language not his own, did not cause the utterances of divine truth to

5. Fifthly, that much of the matter of Holy Scripture is intrinsically incredible. Passing over all other examples of this objection in the past, and in other countries, I will name only the works of Dr. Colenso on the Pentateuch.

6. Sixthly, that the text, by reason of innumerable variations, is uncertain, and that the authority of the Book is thereby shaken; for if the text be uncertain in one part, we do not know that it is not uncertain in others.

I do not at all underrate the importance of meeting these objections, which has been already done again and again in past centuries. But error, as I have said, seems to have periodic times, and to return upon us; not indeed, identical, nor in the same precise forms, but still the same errors under new aspects, and attaching to other portions of the truth. As I do not now attempt to discuss the large questions I have here enumerated, I will do no more than add one or two general reflections.

1. And first it is to be observed, that the Church in

---

become erroneous. The Greek of S. John is not Attic, but his Gospel is free from all error. A Jew of Tarsus might speak Greek rudely, but the matter revealed to him was not thereby infected with human error. The above passages may indeed be quoted against the extreme theory of literal inspiration, but not to prove that the inspired writers were liable to error.

declaring the Vulgate Version to be authentic, does not declare that the existing text is free from uncertainty.

By *authentic*, the Church intends to say *authoritative* in the sense of jurisprudence, in which an 'authentic document' signifies a writing which is conclusive in evidence. Such writings may be of three kinds: 1. *Autographa*, or the original documents; 2. *Apographa*, or copies agreeing with the original; and, 3. *Translations* in versions which are called authentic in a wider sense, conformity of substance with the original being secured.

Again, authenticity is either intrinsic or extrinsic. Intrinsic authenticity in *autographa* signifies that the writing is original, and in the hand of the writer; in *apographa*, or copies, and *translations*, that they are conformable to the original. Extrinsic authenticity is the external evidence by which the intrinsic authenticity is established.

Authenticity is again divided into absolute and relative. 1. *Absolute* authenticity signifies conformity with the original both in matter and form, and in things both of great and of light moment; in a word, in all things which constitute the perfection of the original, to the exclusion of fault or defect. 2. *Relative* or respective authenticity signifies conformity as a whole, but not to the exclusion of lesser faults or defects.

Now, by declaring the Vulgate to be authentic, the Church signifies that it is in conformity with the original Scriptures, and that it has not been vitiated either by the malice or the carelessness of the translators. But theologians of great weight interpret this declaration to signify, that the authenticity is not absolute, extending to jots and tittles, but relative or respective, extending to the substance and to all the chief parts of the text; that is, to the doctrine of faith and morals, and to all the histories, facts, and sayings which are contained in it.

In this sense the Council of Trent declared the Vulgate to be authentic; but in doing so it did not detract from the authenticity of the Greek or the Hebrew Scriptures.[1]

And this is the more evident from the fact that two editions of the Vulgate were published, the one

---

[1] 'I. Vulgata versio Latina est authentica.

'II. Tridentinum duntaxat declaravit, Vulgatam esse respective authenticam, scilicet'in his quæ ad fidem et mores pertinent.

'Obs. Cum in decreto Tridentino hactenus examinato Vulgata solum cum aliis Latinis editionibus comparata declaretur authentica; aperte colligitur per hanc declarationem nihil derogari authentiæ quam græcis Hebraicisque fontibus præter Protestantes multi Catholici et versioni LXX. Interpretum contra priores plerique postremi tribuunt.'—*Theol. Wirceburg.* tom. i. pp. 26, 35.

by command of Sixtus V., the other of Clement VII., with numerous corrections of the text.

It is clear, therefore, that the Church has never pronounced any version to be identical in every jot or tittle with the sacred original.

And this leads us to a train of thought very seasonable at this day. At this moment there exists in the Christian world an almost inconceivable multitude of copies of the Bible, in I know not how many tongues. The art of printing has multiplied them with a rapidity and a profusion which would be almost miraculous not only to a mediæval transcriber, but to Caxton and Aldus. As we trace this wide stream upward through the last three centuries, it becomes narrower and narrower, until we reach the time when printed volumes disappear, and a number of manuscripts—many indeed, but in proportion to the printed copies indefinitely few—is all that represents the written Word of God. If we trace this stream of written tradition upwards, it becomes narrower still. Without doubt, the copies and versions of Scripture were always numerous; and multitudes have perished by age and other causes: multitudes have ceased to exist since the art of printing rendered a manuscript an unwieldy and wearisome book. Nevertheless, the ancient manuscripts are still the chief criteria for the correction of our printed text. And of these none is to be found of an earlier date than the fourth century. Some twenty or thirty principal manuscripts in Greek, and about forty in Latin, are all that appear to remain to us of a trustworthy kind. Of course, I do not forget the texts which are incorporated in the works of the Fathers, and in the Lectionaries or Antiphonaries. But we are now speaking of texts or manuscript copies representing the great and Divine Original, which is now, like the body of Moses, withdrawn by the Divine Providence from the custody of man. This is a wonderful fact; and wonderful also it is that we so little reflect upon it. In the heat of their controversies, men contend as if their Bibles were attested facsimiles, stereotyped or photographed copies of the autograph of S. John and S. Paul; utterly inconsiderate of the long tract of human agency by which the Scriptures have come down to them, and all the while refusing to believe in the Divine office of the Church, which has guarded and authenticated the written Word of God to us by its unerring witness. The authenticity, intrinsic and extrinsic, of each particular writing of the New Testament, was known and guaranteed by those to whom the several inspired writers committed it. The Church, by the interchange of these testimonies, and by the collection of the books so attested, formed the canon, in which it recognised the revelation it had already received, and spread throughout the world, before the canon was collected. The Scripture corresponded with this great Original, as the Tabernacle corresponded afterwards, with the Pattern which was shown to Moses in the Mount. The Church is the sole judge of the intrinsic authenticity, and alone knows the handwriting of the Author of the Sacred Books, and the autograph of the Spirit of God.

The next observation to be made is, that although, by the assistance of the Holy Spirit, the Church both knows, and at all times can declare with divine certainty, the doctrine of faith and morals committed to its charge; and although it can also declare, and has declared with divine certainty, the existence of Holy Scripture, the catalogue or canon of the Sacred Books, the inspiration of the writers—their immunity, and therefore the immunity of their writings, from all falsehood or error,—nevertheless, it has hitherto only declared the Vulgate to be authentic, and that, as I have already shown, with the relative or respective authenticity, which does not exclude the errors of translators or transcribers. It has never as yet declared any text to possess immunity from the errors of translations or transcriptions, nor that transcribers or translators are exempt from the liability to err. The custody of the faith resides in the sphere of the Divine illumination, which pervades the Church with its active and passive infallibility. The custody of the material documents of Holy Scripture resides in the office of the Church, as a Divine witness to the facts of its own history, and of the Divine gifts committed to its trust. The Scriptures were indeed written by an impulse and assistance of God, and as such, are Divine endowments to the Church; but the material volumes, the manuscripts or parchments, were not a part of the deposit, like the Divine truths revealed to the Apostles, nor like the holy sacraments divinely instituted by Jesus Christ.

It follows from what has been said,

1. That whensoever the text can be undoubtedly established, the supposition of error as to the contents of that text cannot be admitted : but,

2. That wheresoever the text may be uncertain, in those parts error may be present.

But this would be not error in Scripture, but in the *transcription* or *translation* of the Scripture, and would be due, not to the inspired writer, but to the translator or transcriber.

That such a supposition may be entertained, is evident from the fact that the variations in the versions are stated by some writers at 30,000, by others at 40,000, by others at 100,000. That variations existed already in S. Augustine's time is evident from his answer to Faustus the Manichæan, to whom he says, 'If anything absurd be alleged to be there (*i.e.* in Holy Scripture), no man may say, The author of this book did not hold the truth. But (he must say), either the manuscript is faulty, or the translator was in error, or you do not understand it.'[1] In these words S. Augustine has provided an answer for our days as well as for his own. It would seem that these three suppositions suffice to cover the difficulties alleged against the historical character and intrinsic credibility of Holy Scripture.

1. First, it is evident that Holy Scripture does not contain a revelation of what are called physical sciences; and that when they are spoken of, the language is that of sense, not of science, and of popular, not of technical usage.

2. Secondly, no system of chronology is laid down

---

[1] 'Ibi si quid velut absurdum moverit, non licet dicere, Auctor hujus libri non tenuit veritatem: sed aut codex mendosus est, aut interpres erravit, aut tu non intelligis.'—S. Aug. *Cont. Faust.* lib. xi. c. 5, tom. viii. p. 222.

in the Sacred Books. There are at least three chronologies, probable and admissible, apparently given by Holy Scripture. It cannot be said, therefore, that there are chronological faults in Holy Scripture, forasmuch as no ascertained chronology is there declared.

3. Thirdly, historical narratives may appear incredible and yet be true; and may seem irreconcileable with other history, and yet the difficulty may arise simply from our want of adequate knowledge. A history may seem improbable, and yet be fact after all.

The most certain and exact sciences have residual difficulties which resist all tests, and refuse all solution. The sciences most within our reach, of the natural order, and capable of demonstration, not only have their limits, but also phenomena which we cannot reconcile. How much more Revelation, which reaches into a world of which eternity and infinity are conditions, and belongs to an order above nature and the reason of man! It is no wonder that in the sphere of supernatural science there should be residual difficulties, such as the origin of evil, the freedom of the will, the eternity of punishment. They lie upon the frontier, beyond which, in this world, we shall never pass. Again, what wonder that the Holy Scriptures should contain difficulties which yield to no criticism, and that not only in the sphere of supernatural truth, but also of the natural order—that is, of history, chronology, and the like! To hear some men talk, one would suppose that they were eye-witnesses of the creation, observers of the earth's surface before and after the Flood, companions of the patriarchs, chroniclers of the Jewish race. The history of the world for four thousand years, written in mere outline, with intervals of unmarked duration—genealogies which cannot be verified by any other record, events which are the $\mathit{ἅπαξ\ λεγόμενα}$ of history—may well present difficulties, and apparent improbabilities upon the surface, and yet after all be true. The same historical event, viewed from different sides, will present aspects so different, that the records of it may be apparently irreconcileable; and yet some one fact or event not preserved in the record would solve and harmonise all. It may be from 'intellectual obtuseness,' or 'want of the critical faculty,' or 'obstinate adherence to preconceived belief,' but it makes little impression on me to be told that S. Stephen, in Acts vii. 16, fell into an historical error in saying that Jacob was buried in Sichem. I confess that I cannot explain the difficulty, and that the explanations usually given, though possible and even probable, are hardly sufficient. Nevertheless, I am not shaken in the least as to the divine axiom, that Holy Scripture is exempt from all error. Whether it be a fault in the manuscript, or in the translator, or only a want of our understanding, I cannot tell; but an error in Scripture most assuredly it is not, and our inability to solve it, is no proof that it is. There it stands, an undoubted difficulty in the existing text—and not the only one; and yet all together will not shake our faith in the immunity from error which was granted to the sacred writers.

Nor, again, when we read in one place that King Solomon had 4,000 stalls for horses, in another 40,000; nor that king Josias began to reign at eight years of age, in another place at eighteen. I cannot explain it. But I can imagine and believe many solutions except one, namely, that the inspired writers contradicted themselves, or that in this they were not inspired.

So likewise, when I am told that the history of the Pentateuch is intrinsically incredible;—that half a million of men could not be slain in one battle; that the people in the wilderness could not have survived without water; that to furnish the paschal lambs would require I know not how many millions of sheep; that, according to sheep-masters in Yorkshire and Natal, this would require I know not how many millions of square acres of grass; that the priest could not carry every day a bullock, with his head, and hide, and inwards, and appurtenances, six miles out of the camp, and the like;—I confess that it makes little impression on me. It reminds me of the Athenian, who having a house to sell, carried about a brick in his pocket as a view of the premises; and of another, who showed in his olive garden the well out of which his forefathers used to drink; to which his friend—testing history by mensuration, and yet believing—said, 'What long necks they must have had!' I do not profess to be able to understand all the difficulties which may be raised. The history shows to me afar off like the harvest-moon just over the horizon, dilated beyond all proportion, and in its aspect unnatural; but I know it to be the same heavenly light which in a few hours I shall see in a flood of splendour, self-evident and without a cloud. So I am content to leave, as residual difficulties, the narratives which come down from an age, when as yet the father of secular history had not been born. Why should we assume that we must render an account of all difficulties in Scripture any more than in revelation, or in revelation any more than in science? Why should we be ashamed of saying with

S. Augustine, 'Let us believe and immoveably affirm that in Scripture falsehood has no place.'[1] 'As for us, in the history of our religion, upheld by Divine authority, we have no doubt that whatsoever is opposed to it is most false, let the literature of the world say what it will of it.'[2] 'We cannot say the manuscript is faulty, for all the corrected Latin versions have it so; nor that the translator is in error, for all the corrected Greek have it so. It remains that you do not understand it.'[3] 'Even in the Holy Scriptures themselves, the things of which I am ignorant are many more than the things which I know.'[4] 'Adore in the Gospel what you do not as yet understand, and adore it all

---

[1] 'Ego enim fateor caritati tuæ, solis eis Scripturarum libris qui jam canonici appellantur, didici hunc timorem honoremque deferre, ut nullum eorum auctorem scribendo aliquid errasse firmissime credam. Dum tamen a scribentibus auctoribus sanctarum Scripturarum et maxime canonicarum inconcusse credatur et defendatur omnino abesse mendacium, . . . mentiendi utique non est locus.'—S. Aug. *ep*. 82 *ad Hier*. tom. ii. pp. 190, 198.

[2] 'Nos vero in nostræ religionis historia, fulti auctoritate divina, quidquid ei resistit, non dubitamus esse falsissimum, quomodo libet sese habeant cetera in sæcularibus literis.'—*De Civ. Dei*, lib. xviii. cap. 40, tom. vii. p. 522.

[3] 'Proinde, quia ex apostoli Pauli canonicis, id est, vere Pauli epistolis, utrumque profertur, et non possumus dicere, aut mendosum esse codicem, omnes enim Latini emendati sic habent; aut interpretem errasse, omnes enim Græci emendati sic habent: restat ut tu non intelligas.'—*Cont. Faust.* lib xi. cap. 6, tom. viii. p. 222.

[4] 'Quòd non solum in aliis innumerabilibus rebus multa me latent, sed etiam ipsis sanctis Scripturis multo nesciam plura quàm sciam.'—*Ad Inquis. Januar. Ep. LV*. tom. ii. p. 113.

the more in proportion as it is now hidden from you.'[1] These may be hard sayings to the nineteenth century; but they are the judgments of reason illuminated by faith, 'which is yesterday, and to-day, and the same for ever.'

And if it should seem irrational and perverse to shut our eyes to difficulties, as men say, we can but answer—We neither derive our religion from the Scriptures, nor does it depend upon them. Our faith was in the world before the New Testament was written. The Scripture itself depends for its attestation upon the Witness who teaches us our faith, and that Witness is Divine. Our faith rests upon an order of divine facts which was already spread throughout the world, when as yet the Gospel of S. John was not written. Of what weight are any number of residual difficulties against this standing, perpetual, and luminous miracle, which is the continuous manifestation of a supernatural history among men; a history, the characters, proportions, and features of which are, like the order to which it belongs, divine, and therefore transcend the ordinary course of nations and of men? One of these divine

---

[1] 'Honora in eo quod nondum intelligis; et tantò magis honora, quantò plura vela cernis. . . . Vela faciunt honorem secreti: sed honorantibus levantur vela.'—*Serm. LI. de. Concor. Matt. et Luc.* tom. v. p. 285.

facts, and that which is the centre and source of all our certainty, is the perpetual Voice of the Church of God. That Voice has declared to us that the Sacred Books were written by inspiration, and that whatsoever those books contain, howsoever it may surpass the bounds of our experience, and refuse the *criteria* of our statistics, and the *calculus* of our arithmetic, is simply to be believed because it is divinely true.

CHAPTER IV.

THE RELATION OF THE HOLY GHOST TO THE INTERPRETATION OF SCRIPTURE.

In the last chapter we have endeavoured to ascertain, according to the tradition of the Catholic faith and theology, the relation of the Holy Spirit to the letter and to the substance of Holy Scripture. We may now go on to trace the relation of the same Divine Person to its interpretation.

At the close of the last chapter, it was affirmed that Christianity was neither derived from the Scriptures of the New Testament, nor is dependent upon them: that it was derived from, and that it still depends upon the order of divine facts introduced into the world by the Incarnation; among which facts, one is the perpetual presence of a Divine Teacher among men. In the present chapter, then, we will trace the relation of this Divine Teacher to the interpretation of Scripture. The faith teaches us that what the presence of the Incarnate Son in the years of His ministry was to the Scriptures of the Old Testament, that the presence of the Holy Ghost is, *servata proportione,* to the Scriptures of the New. Now, the Jews were not more unconscious of the presence of a Divine Person among them than the multitude of men at this day.

We read in the fourth chapter of S. Luke's Gospel that on a certain Sabbath day our Lord 'went into the synagogue, according to His custom,' and that ' He stood up to read.'[1] The Sabbath rose upon Nazareth that day like any other, and the people of Israel went to their synagogue as at other times. Jesus was there, according to His custom; and He stood up to read as others were wont to do. The Book of Esaias the prophet was given to Him; and as He unrolled it, He found the place where it was written, ' The Spirit of the Lord is upon me. Wherefore He hath anointed me to preach the Gospel to the poor.' 'And when He had folded the book, He restored it to the minister and sat down.' Then He said: ' This day these words are fulfilled in your ears.' That day was a day of visitation. The Messiah was come, but they knew Him not. With the Scriptures in their hands, they did not recognise the Divine Person of whom the

[1] S. Luke iv. 16-19.

Scriptures spoke. He was come fulfilling the prophecies; but they believed Him to be the carpenter, the son of Joseph. There was a Divine Teacher in the midst of them, but they thought His voice was human. He interpreted to them the sense, and confirmed the authenticity of the Books of Moses and of the Prophets with a Divine witness; but they rejected both His testimony and His interpretation. With the Books of the Law in their hands, they rejected the Lawgiver, and appealed from Him to it, from the living voice of a Divine Teacher to the letter of the Scriptures, interpreted by their own human commentaries. It is of this perversity S. Paul says, 'The letter killeth, the Spirit quickeneth.'[1] S. Augustine says, 'The Jew carries the volume, by which the Christian believes.'[2] Now, was this a transient visitation, or is there still in the midst of us a Divine Person—the living Interpreter of the Holy Scripture—the Guardian both of the letter and of the sense of Holy Writ?

This is a vital question—vital at all times—most vital now in England. Because hitherto England has preserved two things; not wholly, indeed, but with

---

[1] 2 Cor. iii. 6.

[2] 'Codicem portat Judæus, unde credat Christianus.'—S. Aug. *Enarr. in Ps.* lvi. tom. iv. p. 534.

less of mutilation than other Protestant countries; namely, a belief that Christianity is a divine revelation, and that the Holy Scripture is an inspired Book. These have been hitherto the foundations of English Christianity. But they have been secretly and silently giving way. At the present day, many reject Christianity altogether; and many who profess to believe in Christianity reject the inspiration of a large part of the Scriptures. And these things are the forerunners of a flood which has already swept the belief in Christianity and in the Scriptures from the greater part of Lutheran Germany. If Luther should rise from the dead, he would not recognise his own work nor his own posterity. And in Germany there appear to be no signs of rising again from this spiritual death. In France, some seventy years ago, a flood of infidelity burst upon the land, and carried all before it. The Church was swept away. An infidel empire reigned not only by force, but by infidel philosophy, and by infidel education. But France has risen again from the dead, and Christianity and the Church in France is restored to all its power and purity. Its hierarchy, priesthood, and religious are more vigorous and faithful than ever. And despite of indifference and infidelity in individuals, the French people, as a people, are

Christian in faith and works. What has saved France but the Church of God—the supernatural witness, endowments, and power of the holy Catholic and Roman Church? But what shall save England from the unbelief which is impending as an inundation? The Reformation has mined the barriers against scepticism and unbelief. Doubt has been generated, age after age, upon every doctrine of Christianity and every book of Scripture. It seems to hang in the atmosphere, and to find its way impalpably into all minds; not of the irreverent and irreligious only, but even of the higher and the better. And what wonder, when pastors and bishops of the Church of England are leaders in this secession from the Truth? Is there then no power of rising again for England? Is it like Germany, or like France? Is there any barrier to unbelief? any witness for divine faith present in this country to raise it again from the ruin into which the flood of unbelief is visibly bearing it away? I believe there is. Narrow and hardly visible as it now may seem, nevertheless as the legal Christianity of England dissolves and passes away, the Catholic and Roman Church spreads itself with a steady and irresistible expansion. It is indeed a wonderful reverse to human pretension and to human pride, to see at this hour the Catholic and

Roman Church in England standing out as the one and only consistent and inflexible witness and keeper of Holy Writ, the sole guardian of Scripture, both of its sense and of its letter, and therefore the only Scriptural Church, teaching the only Scriptural religion to the English people.

It seems hardly necessary to say that Christianity was not derived from Scripture, nor depends upon it; that the master error of the Reformation was the fallacy, contrary both to fact and to faith, that Christianity was to be derived from the Bible, and that the dogma of faith is to be limited to the written records of Christianity; or in other words, that the Spirit is bound by the letter; and that in the place of a living and Divine Teacher, the Church has for its guide a written Book.

It is to this fallacy I would make answer by drawing out what is the relation of the Holy Spirit to the interpretation of the written Word of God.

I. First, then, it is evident that the whole revelation of Christianity was given by the Spirit of God, and preached also and believed among the nations of the world before the New Testament existed. The knowledge of God through the Incarnation, and the way of salvation through grace, was revealed partly by our Divine Lord, and fully by the Holy Ghost at

His coming. The faith or science of God was infused into the apostles by a divine illumination. It was not built up by deduction from the Old Testament, but came from God manifest in the flesh, and from His Holy Spirit. It was in itself the New Testament, before a line of it was written. It was a Divine science, one, full, harmonious and complete from its central truths and precepts to its outer circumference. It was traced upon the intelligence of man by the light which flowed from the intelligence of God. The outlines of truth as it is in the Divine Mind, so far as God was pleased to reveal, that is, to unveil it, were impressed upon the human mind.

This truth was preached throughout the world by the apostolic mission. They were commanded to 'preach the Gospel to every creature,' and 'to make disciples of all nations.' And what Jesus commanded, the apostles did. They promulgated the whole of Christianity. They baptized men into the faith of Jesus Christ. But before they baptized any man he became a disciple: that is, he learned the faith. The Faith was delivered to him in the articles of the Baptismal Creed, as the law was delivered in the Ten Commandments. These two summaries contain the whole truth and law of God. And every baptized person, according to his capacity, received the explicit knowledge of all that is implicitly contained in them. But what was the source of this perfect science of God in Jesus Christ? It was no written Book, but the presence of a Divine Person illuminating both the teachers and the taught.

And this universal preaching of the apostles was written by the Spirit upon the intelligence and heart of the living Church, and sustained in it by His presence. The New Testament is a living Scripture, namely, the Church itself, inhabited by the Spirit of God, the author and writer of all revealed Truth. He is the *Digitus Paternæ dexteræ,* 'the finger of the right hand of the Father,' by whom the whole revelation of the New Law is written upon the livin tables of the heart. S. Irenæus, the disciple of Polycarp, the disciple of S. John, writing fifty years after the death of the last apostle, asks: 'What if the apostles had not left us writings, would it not have been needful to follow the order of that tradition which they delivered to those to whom they committed the churches? to which many of the barbarous nations who believe in Christ assent, having salvation written without paper and ink, by the Spirit in their hearts, sedulously guarding the old tradition.'[1]

[1] 'Quid autem si neque Apostoli quidem Scripturas reliquissent

This was a hundred and fifty years after the Incarnation. During all this time, which is nearly four generations of men, on what had Christianity depended for its perpetuity but upon the same Divine fact which was its source, the presence of a Divine Person inhabiting the mystical body or Church of Jesus Christ, and sustaining the original revelation in its perfect integrity?

II. But, secondly, this revelation was also divinely recorded before the New Testament Scriptures were written.

It was written, as I have said, upon the mind of the pastors, or the *Ecclesia docens*, the Church teaching the world; and upon the mind of the flock or the *Ecclesia discens*, the Church learning throughout the world.

It was recorded and incorporated in the Seven Sacraments of Grace, which are, each one of them, Truths of revelation permanently embodied and proposed to faith. The sacrament of Baptism incorporates, so to say, the doctrines of original sin and of re-

nobis, nonne oportebat ordinem sequi traditionis, quam tradiderunt iis quibus committebant ecclesias? Cui ordinationi assentiunt multæ gentes barbarorum eorum qui in Christum credunt, sine charta et atramento scriptam habentes per Spiritum in cordibus suis salutem, et veterem traditionem diligenter custodientes.'—S. Iren. *Cont. Hær.* lib. iii. . v. p. 178.

generation; the sacrament of Penance, the absolution of sin after Baptism, the cleansing of the Precious Blood, the power of contrition, the law of expiation; the sacrament of Confirmation, the interior grace and the seven gifts of the Holy Ghost; the sacrament of Order, the divine authority, unity, and power of the Hierarchy of the Church; the sacrament of Matrimony, the unity and indissolubility of Christian marriage, the root of the Christian world; and so on. Each one embodies, teaches, and requires faith in a constellation of Christian truths; and the Seven Sacraments of the Church are a Record, or Scripture of God, anterior to the written Gospels of the Evangelists. Much more, the Divine worship of the universal Church, of which one of these seven Sacraments is the centre, namely the sacrifice and sacrament of the Body and Blood of Jesus Christ. The incarnation, redemption, and consubstantial union of the Mystical Body with its Head, the communion of saints and of souls departed, are therein incorporated and manifested. All truths congregate around the altar, as all truths radiate from Jesus Christ. The whole revelation of Christianity is reflected in it.

But the Church, its sacraments, and its worship were spread throughout the world before as yet the books of the New Testament were written.

It was not till the faith had been everywhere preached, believed, defined in creeds, recorded in the mind of the universal Church, embodied in sacraments, and manifested in its perpetual worship, that the New Testament was formed. By the inspiration and impulse of the same Divine Teacher who had already revealed the whole Truth to the apostles, it was for the most part put in writing. I say for the most part, because the written Scripture is not coextensive with the Revelation of Pentecost, nor with the preaching of the apostles. The written Scripture presupposes and recognises in those to whom it is addressed the knowledge of the whole Truth. It is to the Church, guided by the Spirit of God, what the writings and letters of a man are to his personal identity. They would recognise all, but record only a part; imply many things, and express only such things as fall within their scope.

The most elementary knowledge of Christian history is enough to prove this. The first Gospel, that of S. Matthew, was not written till five years after the ascension, and then in Hebrew only. In Greek it did not exist for five or six years later; that is, for ten years at least, none of the four Gospels, as we possess them, were written. The second Gospel, that of S. Mark, was written about the same time. The third, twenty-four years after. For the first twenty years there were only two Gospels, and those in Greek. The fourth Gospel, that of S. John, was not written till about sixty years after the ascension. Where then, till the end of the first century, or for two generations of men, were the four Gospels, which people seem to imagine were distributed by the twelve Apostles to their converts on the day of Pentecost?

The earliest of the Epistles was written about fifteen years after our Lord's ascension—the latest more than thirty years after that event.[1] But all these books are limited in their scope. Even the four Gospels treat only of the incarnation and earthly life of Jesus. The Book of Acts is but a fragment of the history of S. Peter and S. Paul. The Epistles are local and occasional, and even private and personal in their nature. And all these books for generations were known only by those parts of the Church to which they were dedicated and entrusted. They were not collected into a volume, that is the New Testament, as men call it, did not exist until a hundred years at least after the ascension. During all this century, martyrs, confessors, saints and penitents multiplied in all the world. The apostolic mission

---

[1] The following are the dates of the Books of the New Testament, according to the ordinary Catholic and Protestant authorities.

had become a universal tradition. The Church on earth rested on the sunrise and the sunset, upon Spain, and upon India. The Heavenly Court had already received the saints of three generations of men. But during all this time what was the source of their Christianity, and what its support? Certainly no book, not even the New Testament Scripture, but the New Testament 'in spirit and in truth,' the revelation of the day of Pentecost, given and sustained by the presence of the Holy Spirit in the

Either will equally establish the argument of the text, as they differ but very slightly.

	Rheims Eng. Vers.	Horne's Introd to the Script.
	A.D.	A.D.
S. Matthew	39	38
S. Mark	43	61
S. Luke	57	63
S. John	96	97
The Acts	63	63
Romans	57	58
1 Corinthians	57	57
2 Corinthians	57	58
Galatians	56	53
Ephesians	62	61
Philippians	62	62
Colossians	62	62
1 Thessalonians	52	52
2 Thessalonians	52	52
1 Timothy	66	64
2 Timothy	66	65
Titus	66	64
Philemon	—	62
Hebrews	62	62

Church, the divine and perpetual Teacher of the world. This is the original, of which the written Scripture is but a partial and subsequent transcript, recognising, indeed, the whole circle of divine truths and the whole order of divine facts in the faith and Church of God upon earth, but reciting only portions, and pointing to the living and Divine Teacher as the only guide into all truth.

III. From this it follows further, that this science of God, incorporated in the Church, is the true key to the interpretation of Scripture. It was in possession throughout the world; it was perfect everywhere before the books of the New Testament were written. It bore witness to the whole revelation of the day of Pentecost; it fixed the meaning of the Scriptures by the evidence of divine facts.

The Socinians and Unitarians tell us now, as the Arians and Sabellians told us of old, that the doctrine of the Holy Trinity is not to be read in the New Testament; but it was preached and believed throughout the world before the New Testament was written.

Presbyterians, Independents, and other Protestants tell us now, as the Acephali and others told us of old, that a hierarchy, an episcopate, and a priesthood are not to be found in the New Testament; but there was a hierarchy ruling over the pastors of the

Church, an episcopate feeding the flock, and a priesthood offering the holy sacrifice at the altar among all nations of the world before the New Testament existed.

There are Puritans of every shade and Anglicans of many opinions, who tell us that the Church is an invisible body seen only by faith and by God; that its unity is only moral, not numerical; that it is divisible into many parts, or branches, and that the New Testament does not exhibit the Church as visible to the eye, numerically one, and indivisible in its unity. But before the New Testament was, the Church had expanded from east to west, visible by its organisation, absolute and exclusive in its unity, which the divisions and apostasies of men could neither divide nor multiply.

We are told that there are only two sacraments of the new law, and that they do, or do not confer grace, according as the multiplicity of Protestant errors is pleased to opine; that there is no sacrifice under the Gospel, no real and personal presence of Jesus in the Holy Eucharist. But the Christians throughout the world had received and professed their faith in the seven sacraments of grace, and the perpetual sacrifice and universal presence of the Word made flesh in the Holy Eucharist had already filled the Church with the consciousness of a Divine manifestation before as yet the canon of the New Testament was completed.

Finally, we are told that in the New Testament there is to be read no successor of S. Peter, no vicar of Jesus Christ. But before the New Testament was collected and diffused, all the world recognised one pastor as chief over all, reigning in the place of Peter from his See in Rome.

The faith and the Church then were the key of interpretation. They who read the New Testament, read it in the light of the day of Pentecost and within the circle of the universal Church in which they beheld the order of divine truths or facts, which the New Testament Scriptures recognise and presuppose. This was both the actual and the scientific key to their true interpretation.

IV. From this it is further evident that the Church is the guardian both of the faith and of the Scriptures.

It received both from its divine Head. And it alone received the custody of the divine revelation and of its inspired books. It received from the Church of old, the books of the old law confirmed by the divine witness of Jesus himself; from the synagogue, the later books; and from the evangelists and apostles, their inspired writings, of which it knew the authenticity and genuineness both by extrinsic and intrinsic evidence.

And as the Church alone received both the faith and the Scriptures, it alone witnesses to both, and that with a twofold evidence; first with a human and historical testimony, resting upon its own personal knowledge of the authenticity of those books, an evidence abundant to attest their veracity; and secondly with a divine and supernatural testimony, resting upon its own spiritual consciousness of the truth contained in those books. The witness therefore of the Church is twofold, natural and supernatural, human and divine: sufficient in the lower, and infallible in the higher sphere of its testimony.[1]

Take it even on the lowest ground. In human jurisprudence the most certain rules of interpretation are to be drawn from the judgments of the learned, the precedents of tribunals and cotemporaneous exposition. The two first are sufficient in most cases,

[1] It is strange to read such words as the following:—'The value of internal evidence—always, perhaps, the foundation of Christian belief everywhere—drawn out into philosophy by Anselm, has now been recognised in theory as well as in practice, in theology as well as in philosophy.'—*Theology of the Nineteenth Century.* Fraser's Magazine, No. CCCCXXII. p. 259. What has generated the internal evidence of Holy Scripture in the mind of the Christian world, but this twofold witness of the Church? and of what avail is the alleged internal evidence apart from the Church, still less opposed to it? The Essays and Reviews are answer enough.

the last is held to be certain as an exponent of the meaning of a law and of the mind of the lawgiver. But in the Church we have all this and more. We have both the judgments of doctors and the decrees of councils; and we have more than this, the cotemporaneous exposition of the books of the New Testament by the divine facts which existed before the Scriptures, and are the key to their sense—the Faith, the Church, and the Sacraments spread throughout the world.

The tradition of the Church, then, contains in it all the principles of certainty which govern the science of human jurisprudence. But it contains more. The tradition of the Church is not human only, but also divine. It has an element above nature, the presence of a divine illumination, so that not only the testimony but the discernment of the Church is supernatural. It delivers to us both the original revelation and the Scripture with an infallible certainty, and we receive both from the Church by an act of divine faith.

V. And this brings us to a last truth, that the Church is not merely the interpretation but the interpreter, and is divinely guided in applying this key to the Holy Scriptures. Before the New Testament was written, it was the living witness for the truth, the organ of the Divine and perpetual voice, which in all nations declared the original revelation. Its authority as a teacher rests upon its commission and its infallibility, that is upon the command of its Divine head, and the assistance of the Holy Ghost. The theory that the Church can err could only arise in minds which have lost the faith of what the Church is. Can it be believed that the mystical body of Christ which is indissolubly united to its Divine Head in heaven, should go about on earth teaching falsehoods in His name? Is it credible that the Church, which is the dwelling-place of the Spirit of Truth, should wander from the revelation which radiates from His presence as light from the sun? The Church in the beginning knew the whole revelation of God, and knows it in every age with a perception which is never obscured, and a consciousness which is never suspended. The illumination which pervades its intelligence, unites with the inspiration of the New Testament as two lights pass into one.

The Church diffused throughout the world, both pastors and people are filled by a consciousness of this faith. And in the light of this consciousness the whole sense of Scripture, I do not say in all its contents, but in all that bears upon the faith and law of God, is instinctively clear to it. The indissoluble union between the Holy Ghost and the mystical body secures to it in all ages its passive infallibility in believing. The Church congregated in council has a special assistance to discern and to declare the original revelation, and therefore the sense of Scripture, so far as that revelation is contained in it or reflected by it. The Episcopate has the grace or unction of truth, and when assembled in council has a special assistance and direction in its judgments. General councils are infallible because the Church is so. They are the organs of its discernment and its decrees.

And what is true of the Church as a whole, and of councils as its organs, is true also of its head. The endowments of the body are the prerogatives of its head, who is the centre of the Divine tradition, and the focus of its supernatural illumination. The head of the Church has also, as we have already seen, a twofold relation, the one to the whole body upon earth, the other to its Divine Head in Heaven, which invests him with an eminent grace and assistance of the Holy Spirit, whose organ he is to all the Church and to all the world. The accumulation of all the evidence, human and divine, and of all the lights, natural and supernatural, by which the revelation of God is known or declared, and the books of Holy Scripture, both in their letter and their sense, are guarded and authenticated, resides by a special endowment in the visible head of the Church on earth.

Do I seem to be making a large claim in behalf of the Vicar of Jesus Christ? Does not every one who rejects the living voice of the Church virtually make the same claim for his sect and for himself? He disclaims infallibility, but he is confident that he is in the right: that the Catholic interpretations of the Scripture are erroneous, and his are certain. Churches that are fallible, it seems, never err, at least in their own esteem; and all the multiplication of their perpetual contradictions fails to bring them to a sense of their aberrations. It is strange on what suicidal arguments men will rest themselves. At one time they say that Scripture is so clear and self-evident in its teaching that no humble mind can fail to see its true meaning. If so, why do they contradict each other and themselves at different times? And if so clear, is it not equally so to the Christians of all races and ages who in it have unanimously read the Catholic and Roman faith?

Again, it is said that the reason is enough to discern the true meaning of the Bible. Why, again, are they who hold this principle in irreconcilable conflict?

And if the individual reason is a sufficient criterion of the sense of Scripture, is not the reason of S. Thomas, or of Suarez, or of Bellarmine to be trusted, much more the collective reason of the Church of all ages and of all people upon earth?

Once more, it is said that there is a special promise that all who read the Scripture with prayer, should be led into all truth. Again, the truth is but one; why do they who go by this rule interminably contradict each other? But did not S. Augustine, and S. Athanasius, S. Chrysostom, and S. Cyril of Alexandria read Holy Scripture with prayer to understand it? Have not the saints in all ages? Have they not received the supernatural guidance and instruction promised, as we are told, to all? Do they not all agree in every jot and tittle of the doctrines declared by them as the sense of Holy Scripture? And is not the unanimous consent of the saints the sense and voice of the Spirit of God? Certainly if there be a promise of guidance into the sense of Scripture made to individuals, the same is enjoyed by the saints one by one, much more by them altogether, still more by the whole Church of God, whose collective illumination is a perpetual emanation from the presence of the Spirit of Truth.

Such then is the assertion with which I set out. There is among us now, as there was in the beginning, a Divine Person, the author and teacher of the whole revelation of Christianity, the guardian of the Sacred Books, and the interpreter of their sense: and the Church in all ages, one and undivided, is the perpetual organ of His voice.

From all that has been said it follows that the Scriptures separated from the Church perish. The appeal from the living voice of the Church to the letter of Scripture destroyed the Divine custody of the letter and of the sense of the Sacred Books. It has needed centuries to unfold the whole reach of this false principle, but it has most surely borne its fruits. The canker fastened upon the root, and has been spreading in secret through the sap to the trunk, and throughout the spread of the branches even to the utmost spray.

First, the interpretation of Holy Scripture was lost in the contradictions and confusions of human teachers. And when the right sense is lost, the Scripture is lost. Just as a man's will is his will only in the sense intended by him, and in no other: and his will ceases to be his will when it is interpreted against or beside his intention. S. Jerome says,[1] 'The Gospel consists not in Scriptures, but in the sense; not on the surface, but in the marrow; not in the foliage of words, but in the root of truth.' Again, he says, 'The Divine Scriptures when misinterpreted by men become human.' So that, after all, the most scriptural are often the most unscriptural. Vincent of Lerins says that heretics have always been conspicuous for an obtrusive abundance of quotation.[2] S. Augustine calls the texts which human teachers misinterpret, 'the shower of snares,' *pluvia laqueorum*,[3] of which the Psalmist speaks.

But when the interpretation goes, faith in the in-

---

[1] 'Marcion et Basilides et cæteræ 'Hæreticorum postes non habent Dei evangelium: quia non habent Spiritum sanctum, sine quo humanum sit evangelium quod docetur. Nec putemus in verbis Scripturarum esse evangelium, sed in sensu: non in superficie, sed in medulla; non in sermonum foliis, sed in radice rationis. ... Grande periculum est in ecclesia loqui, ne forte interpretatione perversa de evangelio Christi hominis fiat evangelium, aut quod pejus est diaboli.'—S. Hier. *in Gal.* cap i. tom. iv. pp. 230, 231.

[2] 'Hic fortasse aliquis interroget, *an et hæretici divinæ Scripturæ testimoniis utantur*. Utuntur plane, et vehementer quidem, nam videas eos volare per singula quæque sanctæ legis volumina.'—Vinc. Lirin. *Commou.* cap. 25.

[3] 'Non enim Prophetæ tantùm, sed omnes verbo Dei animas irrigantes, nubes dici possunt. Qui cum malè intelliguntur, pluit Deus super peccatores laqueos. ... Et hic igitur eadem Scripturarum nube, pro suo cujusque merito, et peccatori pluvia laqueorum, et justo pluvia ubertatis infusa est.'—S. Aug. *Enar. in Ps. x.* tom. iv. p. 64.

spiration of Scripture speedily follows. The course of Biblical criticism, both in Germany and in England, shows that men do not long believe in the divine inspiration of books which are rendered incredible by misinterpretation.

The school which is becoming dominant in the Anglican Church and in the Universities, by reason of its scholarship and attractiveness, has already rejected the inspiration of large parts of Holy Scripture, and reduced the nature of inspiration to limits far short of the truth.

To deny the inspiration of certain books, or parts of such books, is to deny such documents to be Scripture: that is, to deny the genuineness, authenticity and identity of these books. So 'their speech spreadeth like a canker.'[1] It is come then to this, that the system which founded itself upon the claim to be essentially and above all Scriptural, is ending in denying the inspiration and authenticity of Holy Scripture.

The guardianship of the Church being forfeited by the act of separation from its unity; even the fragmentary Christianity which the separated bodies carried away with them has dissolved, and the Sacred

[1] 2 Tim. ii. 17.

Books have lost the divine evidence of their inspiration and veracity.

What has hitherto been said will both explain and refute two accusations commonly brought against the Catholic Church, the one that it supersedes to so great an extent the use of Scripture in the devotions of its people; the other, that it enunciates its doctrines in an arbitrary and dogmatic way, regardless of the facts of Christian antiquity and history.

Now, as to the former. In one sense it is simply unmeaning and untrue to say that the Church supersedes the use of Holy Scripture in the devotions of its people. Of what is the Missal, the Breviary, the Ritual, and all the public services composed but of the very text of Holy Scripture? Every doctrine of the faith, every sacrament, every festival, is exhibited in the very words of the inspired books. Every doctrine and sacrament becomes the centre round about which the prophecies, types, and fulfilments recorded in Holy Scripture are gathered. They are clothed in a tissue of the inspired words, chosen out and interwoven together with a supernatural discernment and combination. They who by the grace of God have come from the wilderness into the true fold, can perhaps alone fully appreciate the change from the level and dim surface of the Sacred Text as read out of the Church, to the luminous distinctness, the splendour, and the beauty of the very same words when they are proclaimed by the voice of the Church in the acts of its public worship. From every page of Scripture words hitherto passed over seem to rise up as prophets, seers, and evangelists, and to speak with an articulate and living voice of the presence and power of the kingdom of God. It is as if David, and Esaias, the Beloved Disciple, and the Apostle of the Gentiles were speaking to us and worshipping with us. But the objection is perhaps chiefly intended in respect to the private devotions of the people, to whom books of devotion written by uninspired men, rather than the Old or New Testament, are generally given. Now, there is at first sight a semblance of truth in the objection. It is perfectly true that manuals of devotion are distributed rather than Bibles, and for many sufficient and, we should have thought, self-evident reasons.

From what has been already said, it is manifest that the revelation of Divine truth and will was anterior to all Scriptures and independent of them: that it was full, complete, and harmonious in itself: that it was perfect in its unity, order, and relation of truth with truth. But it is equally manifest that the Scripture afterwards written, though it recognises, presupposes and refers back to this revelation, does not contain it as a whole, and what it does contain is to be found, not in order and completeness, but detached and scattered, so to speak, here and there through the Sacred Text, which treats also of local, personal, and transitory events. It is perfectly true, therefore, that the Church puts into the hands of its people books of devotion which represent the whole order and completeness of revelation, and not the partial and unordered aspect of Scripture. Those books contain the Baptismal Creed, which enunciates in compendium the whole dogma of faith; the Divine Law of the Ten Commandments, as perfected by the Gospel, not the extinct Sabbatical injunctions of the Jews; the mysteries of the Holy Trinity, of the Incarnation and Passion; of the Holy Sacraments, their divine intention and supernatural grace, with the practices and counsels of penance and piety, whereby to prepare for their reception, and the like. The Church teaches its people now to worship and adore the Divine Presence in the midst of us, as it did before the Scriptures were written: as it did, too, when the millions of Christendom had no Scriptures in their hands, because the modern invention of printed books was not as yet known, when, too, they could not have read those books even if they had possessed them: which was always the state of the multitude, and probably always will be, to the end of the world. God has prepared for the poor and the unlearned a rule of faith, and a practice of devotion, full, unerring, and compassionately fitted to their needs, anterior in time to all Scriptures, and essentially independent of them. But as the objection is not confined to the poor, so neither must the answer be. And perhaps there can hardly be found a more pointed and exact illustration of the argument of this chapter.

It is certain, then, that the practice of Catholics is not so much to make use of the text of Scripture in their devotions as of devotional books. But of what are those books composed? Take, for example, the whole class of books used for meditation or mental prayer. They are from first to last the text of Holy Scripture expounded and applied. Such books are almost innumerable in the Catholic Church. The spiritual exercises of S. Ignatius, and all the expositions and commentaries upon them, and all the countless volumes of meditations for every day in the year which have sprung out of them, what are all these but Holy Scripture brought home to the people in the minutest and most practical way? Out of the Catholic Church such works hardly exist. English

Protestants have certain Commentaries on Holy Scripture; but these do not supply that which the Catholic Church multiplies and puts into the hands of its people with such abundance, that no thoughtful Catholic is without a book of devout meditation upon Holy Scripture.

I do not here stop to answer the strange and extravagant pretensions of using Holy Scripture 'without note or comment.' It is enough to answer, God has given a note and comment on Holy Scripture which no man can exclude if he would. No man can disregard without sin, the Church, the Faith, the Holy Sacraments, and finally the living Voice of His Spirit speaking through the Church in every age, as in the age before the Scriptures were written.

But, finally, there is one more practical and complete answer to this objection. Catholics readily admit that they do not go to the text of Scripture for their devotion, as others do who are out of the unity of the Church. The reason cannot be better given than in the words which history ascribes to one of our English kings. It is said that Henry III. of England was asked by S. Louis of France why he went so often to mass and so seldom to sermon; he answered: 'Because I had rather speak face to face with my friend, than hear about him.' It is the consciousness of the presence of Jesus, God and man, in the Blessed Sacrament of the Altar which draws all eyes and all hearts round about Him to the point where He is personally present. S. Augustine says that the Scriptures are 'the Epistles of the King' sent to us.[1] But when the King is with us we lay up His Epistles, and speak with Him: as friends read the letters of an absent friend, but turn to him when he is among them. The perpetual, daily, hourly worship and communion with our Divine Master, which is equally intelligible, personal, and all-sufficing to the rich and to the poor, to the learned and to the little child, and indeed more realised and known by the hearts of the poor and of children than by any others—this it is which renders the text of Holy Scripture, loved and honoured as it is, less necessary to the disciples of the Church of Jesus Christ.

The other objection I shall touch but briefly. It is often said that Catholics are arbitrary and positive even to provocation in perpetually affirming the indivisible unity and infallibility of the Church, the primacy of the Holy See, and the like, without regard to the difficulties of history, the facts of antiquity, and the divisions of Christendom. It is

[1] S. Aug. in Psalmos, tom. iv. 1159.

implied by this that these truths are not borne out by history and fact: that they are even irreconcileable with it: that they are no more than theories, pious opinions, assumptions, and therefore visionary and false.

We very frankly accept the issue. No Catholic would first take what our objectors call history, fact, antiquity, and the like, and from them deduce his faith; and for this reason, the faith was revealed and taught before history, fact, or antiquity existed. These things are not the basis of his faith, nor is the examination of them his method of theological proof. The Church, which teaches him now by its perpetual living voice, taught the same faith before as yet the Church had a history or an antiquity. The rule and basis of faith to those who lived before either the history or antiquity of which we hear so much existed, is the rule and basis of our faith now.

But perhaps it may be asked: 'If you reject history and antiquity, how can you know what was revealed before, as you say, history and antiquity existed?' I answer: The enunciation of the faith by the living Church of this hour, is the maximum of evidence, both natural and supernatural, as to the *fact* and the *contents* of the original revelation. I know what are revealed there not by retrospect, but by listening.[1]

Neither is this the Catholic method of theological proof. Let us try it by a parallel. Would those who so argue, try the doctrine of the Holy Trinity by the same method? Would they consider it arbitrary and unreasoning to affirm that God is one in nature and three in person, until we shall have examined the history and facts of antiquity—that is, until we shall have heard and appreciated the Sabellian, Arian, Semiarian, and Macedonian heresies? Or take the doctrine of the Incarnation. Are we to take the Monophysite, Monothelite, and Apollinarian heresies, and modify a doctrine of the Incarnation in conformity to these facts? Was not the doctrine of the Holy Trinity and of the Incarnation revealed, preached, and believed throughout the world before there were Sabellians or Nestorians to deprave these truths? Was not the unity and infallibility of the Church and the primacy of the Holy See instituted and believed throughout the world before Montanists, or Acephali,

[1] No better sample of unconscious Rationalism can be given, though I quote it with regret, than the following words: 'To discern the sacred past by the telescopic power of genius, and by the microscopic power of scholarship, is one of the chief ends for which universities and cathedrals are endowed, and for which theology exists.'—*Theology of the Nineteenth Century.* Fraser's Magazine No. CCCCXXII. p. 256.

or Donatists, or Greeks arose to gainsay these facts? In truth, and at the root, is not this inverted and perverse method a secret denial of the perpetual office of the Holy Ghost? The first and final question to be asked of these controversialists is: Do you or do you not believe that there is a Divine Person teaching now, as in the beginning, with a divine, and therefore infallible voice; and that the Church of this hour is the organ through which He speaks to the world? If so, the history, and antiquity, and facts, as they are called, of the past vanish before the presence of an order of facts which are divine—namely, the unity, perpetuity, infallibility of the Church of God: the body and visible witness of the Incarnate Word, the dwelling and organ of the Holy Ghost now as in the beginning: the same yesterday, to-day, and for ever: its own antiquity and its own history.

Let no one suppose that Catholic theologians, in refusing to follow the inverted and rationalistic method of extracting dogmas from the facts of history, for a moment either abandon the facts of history as insoluble, or conceive that they are opposed to the doctrines of faith. The Fathers were the children and the disciples of the Church. They learned their faith from it, and they expressed it partly in the words the Church had taught them, partly when, as yet, the Church had not fixed its terminology in language of their own. In the former, the Church recognises its own voice; in the latter, it knows their intention even when their language is less perfect. And when they err, the Church both discerns and corrects it: for the Church was their guide and teacher, not they hers. If any one desire to see both proof and illustration of what is here said, let him examine the treatises of Petavius on the Patristic language relating to the Holy Trinity; or, to refer to a more accessible work, let him turn to the language of the Fathers on the Immensity of the Son in a well-known work on the Development of Christian Doctrine. The havoc made not only with the writings of the Fathers, but with the doctrines of faith, by those who profess to interpret them, apart from the lineal tradition of the Church, is evidence enough of the falseness of this method.[1] The only Father in whom, it is said,

---

[1] As a *reductio ad impossibile*, and I may say, *ad absurdum*, the following words suffice: 'We must get rid of our preconceived theories of what the Bible ought to be, in order to make out what it really is. The immense layers of Puritanic, scholastic, papal, and patristic systems, which intervene between us and the Apostolic or Prophetic Ages—the elevation of the point of view on which those ages stand above our own—aggravate the intensity of the effort to the natural sluggishness of the human heart and intellect.'—*Theology of the Nineteenth Century*. Fraser's Magizine, p. 255. It would be

the Church has noted no error, is S. Gregory of Nazianzum. The Church can freely criticise the works of its own disciples: for while they may err, it cannot. And the imperfect conceptions and imperfect definitions of individual Fathers of an early age are rectified by the mature conceptions and authoritative definitions of the Church in a later. The maturity of theology is not antiquity, but its later days; and language which was blameless in earlier and simpler times, may become heterodox in after ages: for example, the procession of the Holy Ghost from the Father through the Son, the Immaculate Nativity of the Mother of God, and the like. Again, language which once was heterodox may become the test of truth, as the Homoousion, which was condemned by the Council of Antioch in the Sabellian sense, and in half a century was inserted in the Creed by the Council of Nice. No critic except the living and lineal judge and discerner of truth, the only Church of God, can solve these inequalities and anomalies in the history of doctrine. To the Church the facts of antiquity are transparent in the light of its perpetual consciousness of the original revelation.

still harder to reconcile the 'immense layers' of this counsel with the simplicity of the Divine action, whereby in all ages, *pauperibus evangelizatur*, 'to the poor the Gospel is preached.'

Lastly, it is evident that in the Church alone the Scriptures retain their whole and perfect meaning. We hear to weariness of 'the Bible and the Bible alone;' but how is it that men forget to add, and ' the right sense of the Bible?' For what can add to, or take from, or mutilate the Bible more profoundly than to misinterpret its meaning? Is it Scriptural to say that 'This is my body' does not signify that it is His body; or 'Whosesoever sins ye forgive' does not convey the power of absolution; or 'Thou art Peter, and upon this rock' does not mean that 'Peter is the rock;' or 'They shall anoint him with oil' does not intend the use of oil? Surely the Scriptural Church is that which takes these words in this sense of the divine facts and sacraments, which were believed and venerated in the world before the Scripture was written.

Nay, more, the Church so honours the written Word of God, that it acts upon its lightest word. It is a strange thing to hear men say that such and such doctrines are incredible because so little is said of them in Holy Scripture. Is truth measured by quantity? How many divine words are needed to overcome the unbelief of men? How often must God speak before we obey Him? How many times must He repeat His revelations before we will submit to His divine voice? Does not every spark contain the whole nature of fire? Does not every divine word contain the veracity of God? The Church of God recognises His voice in every utterance, and honours the divine will revealed in the fewest syllables. The words 'He that loveth father or mother more than me is not worthy of me,' has filled the world with disciples. 'Whosoever shall lose his life for my sake shall find it,' has multiplied the army of martyrs. 'Whosoever shall confess me before men,' has made the weakest dare the power of the world. 'If thou wilt be perfect, sell all that thou hast,' has created the state of voluntary poverty. The twenty-fifth chapter of S. Matthew has filled the Church with the orders of active charity. 'Mary hath chosen the better part,' has created and sustained the life of contemplative perfection. These single words, once spoken, are enough for the disciples of the Church, which is the dwelling of the Holy Spirit of Truth, the Author of the Sacred Books. It is this profound faith in their sacredness which made S. Paulinus lay them up in a tabernacle by the side of the Tabernacle of the Blessed Sacrament; and S. Edmund kiss the page of the Bible both before and after reading it; and S. Charles read it kneeling, with bare head and knees. So the Church cherishes its least jot or tittle, and guards it as a deposit dearer than life itself. And now it is every day becoming manifest that in the flood of unbelief pouring at this time upon England, the sole barrier to the inundation, the sole guardian and keeper of Holy Writ in all the integrity of its text and meaning, the sole divine witness of its inspiration, the sole, immutable, and unerring interpreter of its meaning is the Catholic and Roman Church.

CHAPTER V.

THE RELATION OF THE HOLY GHOST TO THE DIVINE TRADITION OF THE FAITH.

There now remains but one other subject on which I purpose to speak. It has been affirmed in the last chapter that Christianity whole and perfect was anterior to the records of Scripture and independent of them. It remains now to show that Christianity has been preserved 'pure . . . and unspotted from the world,' that the illumination of Divine Truth, in the midst of which the written record lies encompassed as by a living and intelligent light, sustained by a living and Divine Teacher, is at this day as it was when it came from the Father of lights, without change or shadow of alteration. And this we shall see more clearly by tracing the relation of the Holy Spirit to the tradition of the dogma of faith.

But before I enter upon this point I am irresistibly drawn to say a few words on the analogy between the

Church in Rome in the fourth century, and in England in the present.

For three hundred years the mightiest empire the world ever saw strove with all its power to drive the Church of God from off the face of the earth. All that force could do was tried, and tried in vain. The Church withdrew itself, but was still visible. It worshipped in catacombs, but bore its witness by martyrdom. When the storm was overpast, it ascended from the windings of the catacombs to worship in the basilicas of the empire. It must have been a day full of supernatural joy, a resurrection from the grave, when the Christians of Rome met each other in the streets of the city by the light of the noonday sun. In those three hundred years a change altogether divine had passed upon the empire. The world from which the Church withdrew itself was compact, massive, irresistible in its material power, its gross paganism, and its profound immorality. The world which met the gaze of the Church at its rising was altogether changed. Christianity had penetrated on every side. It was in all its provinces, in all its cities, in Rome above all, in its legions, and its fleets, in the forum, in the senate, and in the palace of the Cæsars. The heathen world was dissolving and passing away by the twofold action of an internal disintegration, and of the expansion of the light of faith. The outlines of the Christian world were already traced upon the earth, and its rudiments were rising into visible unity and order. The image of the city of God hovered above the tumults and confusions of mankind, awaiting the time when the Divine will should clear from the circuit of the Roman world that which hindered its peaceful possession.

Like to this in many ways is the change which is now before our eyes. I pass by the history of wrongs and sufferings which are now no more. It is a grievous and fearful tale, to be forgotten, if it may. Let us turn to brighter things. For three hundred years the Church in England has worshipped in secret, withdrawn from the sight of man. After all its wounds it lived on, a vigorous and imperishable life, and came forth once more, ascending from the catacombs to offer the Holy Sacrifice in stately sanctuaries, and the light of noon.

It is now thirty years since it rose again from its hiding-place; and the world which meets its view is far other than the world which drove it before its face. It sees no more the whole people of England, under a dominant hierarchy, armed with the power of law to persecute even to death the priest who offers the holy sacrifice, and to force an outward uniformity upon the whole population. It does not any longer see the Anglican Church sole and exclusive in its privileges, and asserting authority over the English people. The days of its supremacy are long gone. England is now in the possession of a multitude of sects, among which the Church of the Reformation finds its place and its kindred as one among many, richer and more favoured by the higher classes, but content with its wealth and place, and the toleration which it shares with others.

There are signs upon the horizon over the sea. Protestantism is gone in Germany. The old forms of religious thought are passing away. They are going in England. Separation has generated separation. The rejection of the Divine Voice has let in the flood of opinion, and opinion has generated scepticism, and scepticism has brought on contentions without an end. What seemed so solid once is disintegrated now. It is dissolving by the internal action of the principle from which it sprang. The critical unbelief of dogma has now reached to the foundation of Christianity, and to the veracity of Scripture. Such is the world the Catholic Church sees before it at this day. The Anglicanism of the Reformation is upon the rocks, like some tall ship stranded upon the shore, and going to pieces by its own weight and the steady action of the sea. We have no need of playing the wreckers. It would be inhumanity to do so. God knows that the desires and prayers of Catholics are ever ascending that all which remains of Christianity in England may be preserved, unfolded, and perfected into the whole circle of revealed truths and the unmutilated revelation of the faith. It is inevitable that if we speak plainly we must give pain and offence to those who will not admit the possibility that they are out of the faith and Church of Jesus Christ. But if we do not speak plainly, woe unto us, for we shall betray our trust and our Master. There is a day coming, when they who have softened down the truth or have been silent, will have to give account. I had rather be thought harsh than be conscious of hiding the light which has been mercifully shown to me. If I speak uncharitably let me be told in what words. I will make open reparation if I be found in fault.

Now, what I wish to show in this chapter is, that the real ultimate question between the Catholic Church and all Christian bodies separated from it, is not one of detail but of principle. It is not a controversy about indulgences, or purgatory, or invocations and the like, but of the divine tradition of dogma, its certainty and its purity. The Catholic Church teaches that, as the preservation of the world is creation produced, and a continuous action of the same omnipotence by which the world was made, so the perpetuity of revelation is sustained by the continuous action of the same Divine Person from whom it came.

All bodies in separation from the Church justify their separation on the alleged necessity of reforming the corruptions of doctrine which had infected the Church and fastened upon the dogma of faith. But if the same Person who revealed the truth still preserves it, then it is as unreasonable for man to profess to reform the Church of God as it would be to endeavour to uphold or to renew the world. Men may gird a dome, or reform a political society, but they can no more reform the Church of God than they can give cohesion to the earth, or control the order of the seasons or the precessions of the equinox.

God alone can reform His Church, and He reforms it by itself acting upon itself, never by those who refuse to obey it, and oppose its divine voice. God has reformed the Church by its Pontiffs, and its Councils. A great part of the Pontifical law, and the greater part of the decrees of Councils, as, for instance, of Constance and of Trent, are occupied with the reformation not of the doctrines of the Church, but the sins of men. As each man can reform himself alone, so the Church alone can reform itself. But this reformation does not enter into the divine sphere of the faith or law of Jesus Christ, which is always pure and incorrupt, but into the wilderness of human action, human traditions, and the sins which by human perversity are always accumulating.

Now, my purpose is to show that the confusions, contentions, and spiritual miseries which have fallen upon England, and which afflict us all both in public and in private, have come from the pretension of reforming the Church of God. And to do so, it will be enough to show, that God has so provided for His Church as to render such a reformation not only needless but impossible.

S. John writing to the faithful at the close of the first century, says:—'You have the unction from the Holy One, and know all things. . . . Let the unction which you have received from Him abide in you. And you have no need that any man teach you; but as His unction teacheth you of all things, and is truth, and is no lie: and as it has taught you, abide in Him.'[1]

These words plainly affirm :—

1. That they had already received the unction of the Spirit of Truth; and therefore that they had no

[1] 1 S. John ii. 20-27.

need to seek for a knowledge which they did not possess, because they had already received it.

2. That they had no need of human teachers, because they were already under the guidance of a teacher who is Divine.

3. That this unction was not *partial* but *plenary*, and taught them 'all things,' that is the *whole revelation* of the Faith.

4. That this unction is truth, absolute and perfect.

5. That it is 'no lie,' is unmixed with any falsehood, error, or doubt. But this unction is the Holy Ghost, who, as we have abundantly seen in the first chapter, rested first upon the head of our Great High Priest Jesus, the Head of the Church, and from Him descends upon His body, which is the Church, and goes down to the skirts of His clothing, to the least of His members, so long as they faithfully abide in Him their head, through the Church which is His body.

I do not know in what words the infallibility of the Church and the immutability of its doctrines can be more amply affirmed. For they declare—(1.) that by the virtue of the perpetual presence of this unction which is the Holy Ghost, the Church possesses the whole revelation of God; (2.) that it is preserved by Divine assistance, unmixed, and in all its purity; and, (3.) that it is enunciated perpetually through the same guidance by a voice which cannot lie.

Now let us draw out the consequences of this truth.

1. The first is that all the doctrines of the Church to this day are incorrupt. I mean that they are as pure to-day as on the day of Pentecost; and that, because they are the perpetual utterances of the Spirit of Truth, by whom the Church both in teaching and believing is preserved from error. Individuals may err, but the Church is not an individual. It is the body of a Divine head united indissolubly to Him. It is the temple of the Holy Ghost united inseparably to His presence. The illumination of the Spirit informs the collective and continuous intelligence of the Church with adequate and precise conceptions of revealed truth, and the assistance of the Holy Spirit guides and sustains the Church in the adequate and precise enunciation of those conceptions. And this, as we have seen, constitutes the active infallibility of the Church as a teacher, exempt from error because guided by a Divine Person. The Church being the organ of His voice, the articulations are human but the voice is Divine.

To deny this is to deny the perpetuity of truth,

and the office of the Holy Spirit as the perpetual guide of the faithful. But if there be no Divine teacher there is no Divine certainty, and faith descends to opinion based upon human evidence and criticism. But this, as we have seen, is rationalism, incipient or absolute, explicit or implicit.

2. But the doctrines of the Church are not only incorrupt but incorruptible. To be incorruptible is not only a fact but a law of their nature. For this cause we deny the possibility of a reformation of the Church as a witness or teacher of faith and morals. The need of such a reformation can never exist. It is the permanent and incorruptible doctrine of the Church, which is the instrument of all reformation. If it be corrupted, how shall it reform or restore others from corruption? If the salt have lost its savour, wherewithal shall it be salted?

I am not denying the existence of error and corruption in Christendom. There has been enough of all kinds in every age; but they have been the errors and corruptions of individuals, not of the Church. They have existed within the Church till the Church cast them out. They never fastened upon the Divine tradition of dogma, nor mingled themselves in the Divine utterances or enunciations of the doctrines of faith. The errors of individuals cannot prevail against the Church. Individuals depend on the Church, not the Church on individuals. The Church depends on its Divine Head, and upon the perpetual presence of the Divine Person who inhabits it. The Church, therefore, has an independent, absolute, and objective existence. It is a Divine creation depending upon the Divine will alone, the instrument of probation to mankind. It is the Sacrament of Truth which remains always the same whether men believe or no. Just as the Holy Eucharist is always the same in the fulness of its Divine sanctity and grace, even though the priest who consecrates and the multitude who receive it be in sacrilege; and as the light of the sun is always the same in unchanging splendour though all men were blind; so with the truth and sanctity of the Church. No human error can fasten upon the supernatural consciousness of the truth which pervades the whole mystical body, and this passive infallibility preserves the doctrines of the faith whole and incorruptible in every age.

All this is more emphatically true of the Teaching Church. The pastors of the Church may err one by one, but the pastoral body can never err. The chief Pastor is in the midst of them, and they, as His witnesses and messengers, constitute the *magisterium Ecclesiæ,* the authoritative voice of the Church speaking in His Name. Here and there individuals among them, one by one, have erred, but their error has never fastened itself upon the authoritative mind and voice of the Church. Every age of the Church has had its heresy; some ages have had many; almost every heresy has had a pastor of the Church for its author; sometimes a heresy has spread wide both among pastors and flock; multitudes have been infected by it. But the mind and voice of the Church has never changed, never varied by an accent or by an iota. As every age has had its heresy, so every heresy has been cast out; some sooner, some later, some with ease, because they were superficial and weak; some with difficulty, because they were tenacious and strong, like the diseases of a living body, of which some are upon the skin, some in the substance, but all alike are cast out by the vigour of health and life. In this way every heresy has been expelled. What mark did Sabellianism, Arianism, Nestorianism, leave upon the mind or voice of the Church? Not a trace nor a tarnish of falsehood or of evil, but only a new precision of conception and expression, a new definition in the mouth of its pastors, and a more explicit faith in the hearts of its people. The Church is the teacher of the pastors, as the pastors are the teachers of the flock. *Doctores fidelium discipulos Ecclesiæ*, as S. Gregory says, and the collective body of its pastors is the organ of the Holy Spirit of truth, and their voice is the active infallibility of the Church. And the mind and voice of the Church are supernatural. I mean the world-wide and continuous intelligence of the Church of all nations and in all ages, which testifies as a witness both natural and supernatural, to the facts of the Incarnation and of Pentecost; and decides as a judge with a supernatural discernment, and enunciates the whole revelation of God as a teacher having authority because of the divine illumination, the divine certainty, and the divine assistance which abides with it. From what I have said it will be understood how any individuals, people, or pastors may err, and yet their error leave no stain or trace upon the mind and voice of the Church, either in its belief or in its teaching; and how not only the truth in itself is incorruptible, as it must be, and also its revelation, for that is God's act, but likewise its tradition and enunciation in the world, for these also are divine actions within the sphere of the human intelligence and human speech, whereby both the thoughts and words of the Church are divinely assisted to perpetuate the original revelation of the continuous operation of the same Divine Person who revealed the faith to men.

3. But that which is incorruptible is immutable, and the doctrines of the Church are the same to-day as in the beginning. All corruption is change, but not all change corruption: there is a change which destroys, and a change which perfects the identity of things. All growth is change. A forest tree in its majesty of spread and stature, has perfect identity with the acorn from which it sprang, but the change of ages which has passed upon it, perfects its identity by unfolding its stateliness and beauty.

But all decay is change. When the tree of the forest droops its branches, dies, and falls into the dust about its root, this change is corruption.

Now, in this latter sense change is impossible in the doctrines of the Church, for God is not the God of the dead but of the living. His Church is the body of His Son, and has life in itself, and all its doctrines and sacraments are the expressions of the character of His life which quickens it.

Take the history of any doctrine in proof. Trace the dogma of the Holy Trinity from the Baptismal formula to the Baptismal creed, to the definitions of Nice and Constantinople, and to the precision of the creed of S. Athanasius. There is here growth, expansion, maturity, and therefore change, but absolute identity of truth. So again trace the doctrine of the Incarnation from the simple formula, 'the Word was made flesh,' to the definitions against the Monophysites, the Monothelites, the Apollinarians, to the *Cur Deus Homo* of S. Anselm, and the treatises of Suarez; the intellectual conception and verbal expression have received a vast expansion, but the truth is identical, namely, God Incarnate, two perfect natures in one Divine person. Or once more, the doctrine of the Blessed Eucharist in all its aspects as a Sacrament, and as a Sacrifice, and as an object of adoration, is no more than the words 'This is My body,' in the fulness of their intellectual conception. And lastly, the doctrine of the Immaculate Conception is no more than the last analysis in a long series of intellectual processes by which the belief of the whole Church from the beginning in the absolute sinlessness of the mother of God has found its ultimate expression. These four doctrines, as they are propounded now, are identical with the same four doctrines as they were propounded in the beginning. They have been unfolded into more explicit enunciation by a more precise intellectual conception and a more exact verbal expression, but they are the same in all their identity. Just as the gold from the mine is always the same though in the succession of times and dynasties it receive new images and superscriptions. So far, then, truth may grow but never change.

Such, however, is not the case with doctrines which are separated from the unity of the Church and the custody of the Divine Teacher who sustains the Faith. Trace the history of the Holy Trinity from Sabellius to Socinus, or of the Incarnation from Nestorius to Strauss, or of the Holy Eucharist from Luther to the present sacramentarian unbelief which overspreads England; or the article of the One Holy Catholic Church from the Reformation to this day in England alone, and in the Anglican Church only, in which no definition can be obtained whether the Church be visible or invisible, numerically one or only morally one, that is, divisible into many parts and yet called one, though it be a plurality of independent and conflicting bodies. This is change indeed, in which the identity of doctrine is lost. The oak has mouldered and fallen into its dust.

This then is what I mean by the immutability of doctrines. They are identical in number and in kind. Their disc and circumference are now as they were when they were first traced on the minds of the Apostles by the light of the Spirit of God. They have come down to us through all ages, and in the midst of all heresies, illuminating all intelligences and conforming them to the truth, but receiving no tarnish or soil from the human intellect, just as the light of heaven pierces through the mists and pestilences of the world, and is in contact with all its corruptions and impurities without a shadow of stain or alteration.

The doctrines of the Church then are as unmixed as the light; and undiminished in all the perfections of truth, which like Jesus ' is yesterday and to-day, and the same for ever.'

4. And from this a fourth truth immediately follows, that the doctrines of the Church in all ages are primitive. It was the charge of the Reformers that the Catholic doctrines were not primitive, and their pretension was to revert to antiquity. But the appeal to antiquity is both a treason and a heresy. It is a treason because it rejects the Divine voice of the Church at this hour, and a heresy because it denies that voice to be Divine. How can we know what antiquity was except through the Church? No individual, no number of individuals can go back through eighteen hundred years to reach the doctrines of antiquity. We may say with the woman of Samaria, ' Sir, the well is deep, and thou hast nothing to draw with.' No individual mind now has contact with

the revelation of Pentecost, except through the Church. Historical evidence and Biblical criticism are human after all, and amount at most to no more than opinion, probability, human judgment, human tradition.

It is not enough that the fountain of our faith be Divine. It is necessary that the channel be divinely constituted and preserved. But in the second chapter we have seen that the Church contains the fountain of faith in itself, and is not only the channel divinely created and sustained, but the very presence of the spring-head of the water of life, ever fresh and ever flowing in all ages of the world. I may say in strict truth that the Church has no antiquity. It rests upon its own supernatural and perpetual consciousness. Its past is present with it, for both are one to a mind which is immutable. Primitive and modern are predicates, not of truth, but of ourselves. The Church is always primitive and always modern at one and the same time; and alone can expound its own mind, as an individual can declare his own thoughts. 'For what man knoweth the things of a man, but the spirit of a man that is in him? So the things also that are of God no man knoweth, but the Spirit of God.'[1] The only Divine evidence to us of

[1] 1 Cor. ii. 11.

what was primitive is the witness and voice of the Church at this hour.

5. But lastly, though the Catholic doctrines are incorrupt, incorruptible, immutable, and therefore always primitive by virtue of the Divine custody and enunciation of the Spirit of Truth, nevertheless they are transcendent; that is, they pass beyond the limits and horizon of our reason, and that because they are truths of the supernatural order. They belong to a world of which all the proportions surpass and overwhelm our powers of thought. They are not discoveries of the reason but revelations of God, and as such, to be received by faith. They must first be believed before they can be understood, for faith generates intelligence. S. Augustine said to the heretics of his day, 'Intellige ut credas verbum meum: sed crede ut intelligas verbum Dei.' 'Understand what I say that you may believe it. Believe what God says that you may understand it.' How should we know the supernatural order, its limits, operations, and doctrines except God had revealed it?

And these truths are but revealed in part, and can therefore only be known in part. They are like the path of a comet which eludes our calculation, or like electricity which renders no account of itself, or like the pencil by which the sun draws the images of nature: all these are facts undoubted, indubitable, yet inexplicable: and, if they were not known scientific truths, would be incredible. So it is with the truths of revelation: for instance, the origin of evil, the freedom of the will under the operation of grace; the end of evil; the eternity of punishment; the solution of the world and of the life of man as a probation for eternity.

And yet these very doctrines, because they are transcendent, are all the more evidently divine. They have the perfection of God upon them. They surpass our finite intelligence, because they are the outlines of truths proportionate to the infinite intelligence. If they presented nothing that I cannot understand, they would present nothing that I might not have invented. 'Credo quia impossibile' is a great truth, though a paradox. If it were possible to man, there would be no need of the revelation of God. The footprint of a man betokens man. The footprints of God point to a Divine Presence as their only cause. The only feet which could impress them are those which walked upon the water. For instance, the doctrine of the Holy Eucharist, of the Communion of Saints, of the Church, one, visible, indivisible, with its supernatural light and divine infallibility, all these point to a wisdom which transcends our reason, as heaven transcends the earth.

Such, then, is the tradition of dogma which descends perpetually in the Church, and such the relation of the Holy Spirit of Truth to that tradition. He is its Author and its Guardian. He both diffuses the light by which it is known and conceived, and presides over the selection of the terms in which it is defined and enumerated.

And here I might leave the subject, but that, in this day, the old pretension of reforming the dogmatic teaching of the Church has been renewed under a more specious form. It is now alleged that the old dogmatic formulas were a true expression of the rude and uncultured religious thought of the early or Middle Ages: that the progress of the human intelligence in the matter of Christian thought demands a new expression; that this expression will not be dogmatic, but 'moral and spiritual;' that the nineteenth century has a theology of its own, which, if not already formed, is forming under intellectual and spiritual impulses, the momentum of which is irresistible. The old Catholic dogmatism is said to be dead and only cumbering the ground. This is a reformation upon the Reformation. All dogmatism—Lutheran, Calvinistic, and

Anglican—must yield to a newer, deeper, more spiritual insight into the moral idea of Christianity. Let us examine these pretensions a little, and then conclude.

In a former chapter I have affirmed that the truths known to the natural reason, or by the light of nature, have been transmitted as an intellectual tradition in the society of mankind. These truths, which relate to the existence and perfection of God, and to the moral nature of man, are permanent and immutable. They constitute what is called natural theology and philosophy. Upon the basis of these certain, fixed, and permanent truths has been raised a structure of metaphysical and ethical systems, which are related to the primary philosophy as dialects are related to a language. Such are the philosophies which have multiplied themselves both before the faith entered into the world and since. Now, these secondary formations or philosophies are, in great part, tentative, uncertain, mutable, and transient. They arise and pass away without at all shaking the permanence of the primary stratum upon which they all repose. The enunciation of these primary truths may be called the axioms or dogmas of philosophy. I affirm that these dogmas of philosophy are fixed and immutable, because the truths they express are so. For instance, the existence of God, His moral perfections, the moral nature of man, his freedom of moral action, his responsibility, and the like, are fixed and immutable truths. They are as true and certain now as they were in the beginning. They can never become more or less true, fixed, or certain, but continue permanently in the same certainty and veracity. For this reason the verbal expression or dogmatic form of them is likewise fixed and permanent. The cry or the pretension of a new philosophy to replace the old, contains a tacit denial of the certainty of these primary truths. It is scepticism under a mask. In the order or sphere of the secondary or deductive philosophies there may be many modifications and steps of progressive exactness. The former are the axioms of the human reason, which stand for ever, like the lights of the firmament, steadfast and changeless.

The same may be said of the scholastic theology, which consists in a scientific treatment of revealed truths, both of the primary and of the secondary order. Those of the primary order are the truths which are expressly revealed; those of the secondary, the conclusions which are deduced from them by process of reasoning.

Now, the former order of primary truths is permanent and immutable. In the secondary order of deductions it is possible that verifications and modifications may from age to age be admitted. But the tradition or transmission of this whole order of truths, both primary and secondary, constitutes the theology of the Church. And this 'Science of God' distributes itself according to its subject-matter into dogmatic, which treats of God and His works in nature and grace; into moral, which treats of the relations of man to God and to his fellows; into ascetical, which treats of the discipline of penance and obedience; and into mystical, which treats of the union of the soul with God, and its perfection. Now, all these four branches of theology have their primary and their secondary truths. The latter spring from the former and repose upon them. In the latter we may conceive of a progressive exactness, always retaining their contact with the primary truths, which are the base of all. But the primary truths are truths of revelation, the knowledge of which resides immutably in the intelligence of the Church. They are fixed truths, and their verbal expressions are fixed dogmas, true in every age, and not less or more true than they were, nor ever will be. For what is dogma but the intellectual conception and verbal expression of a divine truth? But as these truths can never vary, so neither the conception and expression of them. An immutable body casts an immutable shadow. A fixed form describes a fixed outline upon a mirror. The original never varies, therefore the reflection cannot. Of an eternal truth the image must be always the same. For instance, the unity of God is an eternal truth. The proposition that God is One is a dogma; that He is One in nature, Three in person; that the Three Persons are co-equal and co-eternal; that God is infinite in His perfections; that the Father is the fountain of Godhead; that the Son is eternally begotten of the Father alone; that the Holy Ghost eternally proceeds from the Father and the Son, and the like, which might be indefinitely multiplied in enumeration, are eternal truths, and their outlines, reflections and images on the human intelligence, both of the Church and of the individual, are fixed and immutable dogmas.

So again to take another order of truths. That God created the world; that God is present with His creation; that He governs it in the order of nature; that His mind and will are its laws both in their permanent operations and in their exceptional suspension and change—all these are divine truths, and the verbal expressions of them are dogmas; permanent because the truths are immutable, and immutable because true.

Again, that God has redeemed the world; that the Son was made man of a virgin mother; that He lived on earth, taught, worked miracles, chose and ordained apostles, founded His Church, instituted sacraments, died, rose again, ascended into heaven, sent the Holy Ghost to abide and to teach in His stead for ever—all these are both divine truths in their own objective subsistence, in the order of divine facts, and also dogmas in their intellectual conception and verbal expression; and as these truths can never become less true, nor lose their value or place or relation to the will of God, and to the soul of man, so neither can the dogmas which express them.

And lastly, that I may not waste more time over a subject which, but for the almost incredible confusions of thought and language now prevalent, I should not so much as have introduced—that the Church is one and indivisible, singular in existence, the temple of the Holy Ghost, and the organ of His voice; indefectible in its life, immutable in its knowledge of the truths revealed, and infallible in its articulate enunciation of them; that the sacraments are channels of grace, each after its kind; that the operations of the Holy Ghost as the illuminator and sanctifier of the Church and of its members are perpetual: to go no further—all these are divine and permanent and immutable truths, and therefore the intellectual conception and verbal expression of them become fixed and unchangeable dogmas.

What then is dogmatic theology, taken as a whole, with all its contents, but the intellectual conception and verbal expression of the revelation of God, truth by truth, and therefore dogma by dogma; a fixed, permanent, and immutable transcript upon the human mind, and a perpetual and changeless enunciation of the same truth with all its intrinsic truths which constitute its perfect outline and complete integrity?

I can perfectly understand the consistent rationalist when he rejects dogmatic theology, because he disbelieves the whole order of divine truths and facts which it expresses. When the body falls the shadow vanishes. When the original ceases to exist, the reflection passes away. This is intelligible and coherent. Again, when the inconsistent and incipient rationalist rejects those facts of dogmatic theology, or those particular dogmas which express certain particular truths and facts which he disbelieves, this also is intelligible and consistent. But when he, professing to retain a belief in the divine truths and facts of Christianity, denounces dogmatic theology and the tradition of dogma, this in educated and cultivated men is an intellectual obliquity which suggests one of two solutions, either that from want of systematic and orderly study he has only an incomplete and fragmentary knowledge of what dogmatic theology is, or that a warp in the moral habits and temper which influence the intellect, or at least the tongue, makes him less than his own proper stature as a reasoner. And yet this language is not only heard from writers of high name and true cultivation, but is becoming prevalent, and rising into the ascendant at this time.[1]

[1] An instance of this may be seen in a paper entitled *Theology of the Nineteenth Century*, in the number of Fraser's Magazine already quoted, in which the writer, after everywhere denouncing dogmatic theology, especially the scholastic, speaks as follows :—' May I take as an illustration the very corner-stone of Christianity, the Divine subject of the Gospel of history? A common mode of dealing with this sacred topic has been to take certain words—Christ—Messiah—Son of God—Son of Man—two natures—one Person—two wills—one substance, and without defining the meaning of these words, without describing what moral or spiritual truths were intended to be conveyed by them, to arrange them in the most logical way that could be found, and to justify that arrangement by separate Scripture texts' (p. 262). This kind of theology the writer designates as 'barren.' But in this passage the writer seems to show, either that he has never studied dogmatic theology, in which every term such as nature, person, will, substance, &c., has as precise and definite a value as the algebraic symbols; or, that he does not know the limits of dogmatic and mystical theology, under which 'the moral and spiritual truths' are classed and treated.

If such writers and reasoners would only be so good as to state positively what truths and facts of Christianity they do really hold, we should be better able to understand them. But it is to be feared that to extract this confession would lay open a great waste of unbelief which lies hid under a cloud of words. Such a test would inevitably produce one of two consequences. Either it would show that under the rejection of dogmatic theology lies concealed a tacit denial of the Divine truths and facts which it expresses; or that such theologians, when constrained to put into definite words what Divine truths and facts they do believe, would be convicted, within that circle, of being as dogmatic as those they assail. None but obscure or inconsecutive minds can long play fast and loose between affirming Divine truths and denouncing dogmatic theology.

One frequent cause of all this confusion is to be found in the fact, that among non-Catholic writers, above all in England, the distinctions and boundaries of dogmatic, moral, ascetic and mystical theology are lost. Men speak of theology, meaning dogma only; and seem to be unconscious of the other branches of Divine truth, and the separate cultivation which the Church has given to them. Nothing proves this more evidently than the astonishing assertion that a dogmatic treatise on the Incarnation is barren because it does not teach us what was 'the real mind' and 'the delineation of the character' of our Divine Lord:[1] and again, 'It is about as true to say that a human friend raises and benefits us in proportion to the correctness of our theory of his character, as to say that God does so in proportion to the accuracy of our speculative creed.'[2] As a parallel to these statements I would say: 'Astronomical demonstrations are barren because they do not teach us " the real mind," nor " delineate the character " of God. Correct knowledge is useless because it does not alone raise and benefit those who possess it.' Can there be found in all the writers and preachers—out of reverence to the saints, fathers, doctors, theologians of the Catholic Church I will not so much as name them—anyone so senseless as to imagine that dogmatic theology is directed to the delineation of the character of our Divine Master, or that correct intellectual knowledge of the whole science of God without the illumination and correspondence of the heart and will could 'raise and benefit,' if that means sanctify and save, those who possess it? This seems to be a solemn or a superficial

---

[1] *Theology of the Nineteenth Century.* Fraser's Magazine, *ut supra*, p. 282.
[2] Spectator, March 25, 1865, p. 331.

trifling with sacred things; in which men might learn if they had the will, and are therefore culpable, if being ignorant they affect to criticise or to teach. If they would give themselves the trouble to open the first book of elementary theology, they would learn that dogmatic theology is directed to the intellect and mystical theology to the will: that dogmatic theology is said to perfect the intellect because it elevates and informs it with revealed truth, and thereby conforms it to the Divine intelligence in so far as these truths of revelation are known. It is therefore both true and evident that dogmatic theology does most luminously and supernaturally 'raise and benefit' the human intelligence. It makes a man capable of serving God by the 'reasonable service' of faith. Whether he does so or not, depends upon moral conditions, that is, upon the conformity of the will to the dictates of his reason, which has thus been already conformed to the truth and mind of God.

But it is not from dogmatic theology, but from moral theology, that a man must learn the obligations of the Divine will upon the human will. Dogmatic theology enunciates to us the Divine truth: moral theology expounds to us the Divine law. The first formation of the will is accomplished by moral theology. Its maturity is committed to ascetic, its perfection to mystical theology. But these last three provinces of theology, under which falls all that relates to the moral character of God and of our Divine Lord, and all that relates to the interior and spiritual life of God in the soul, and of the soul in God, seem to be wholly unknown to the confident critics of these days. In all the theology, so to speak, of the Anglican Church, I know of no attempt to treat of moral theology or to supply the blank and void which the Reformation has made in this province of the Divine truth, except Andrewes' 'Exposition of the Ten Commandments,' Taylor's 'Ductor Dubitantium,' and Sanderson's 'Cases of Conscience.' And I know of no three works that have fallen into more utter oblivion. The other writings of all three are known, read and quoted, but most rarely are these moral or ethical writings so much as named. And yet Taylor staked his fame on the 'Ductor Dubitantium:' but the atmosphere in which he left it was fatal, and would not suffer it to live. Of the ascetical and mystical theology, excepting Taylor's 'Holy Living and Dying,' what one book can be named which presents a detailed treatment, or so much as an outline, of the spiritual and interior life? And yet it is out of the midst of this barrenness and desolation that the voices are lifted up to denounce dogmatic theology because it does not direct itself to fulfil that which the Church accomplishes with an exuberance of culture in its moral, ascetical and mystical theology, while the Protestant and Anglican systems never accomplish it at all. It is a significant fact that the devotional books in the hands of Protestants are to a great extent translations or adaptations of Catholic works.

Now, I have been led to say thus much in order to preclude certain objections which may be expected to what I have affirmed in this and the previous chapters on the tradition of dogma, and the dogmatic theology of the Catholic Church; and I do so the more carefully, because the scope of this work has hitherto limited our thoughts to the truths of revelation, as they are impressed by the divine intelligence upon the human reason. But it is impossible for me to do more than recognise in passing the vast and wonderful structure of moral wisdom rising from the basis of the revealed perfection and law of God which is contained in the moral theology of the Church. The works of the moral theologians form a library by themselves. One of them alone in his writings has quoted and consulted nearly eight hundred authors of all nations. The elaborate and perpetual study of jurists upon the common and statute law of the realm is a faint analogy of the scientific and exact treatment of the natural and revealed law of God by the councils and theologians of the Church; which, in expounding that law, has a divine assistance guarding it from error.

Of the ascetical theology I will not here attempt to speak; but if any one will trace down the line of writers from S. Nilus and Cassian to the present day, who have treated specifically and in minute detail of the way and instruments of conversion and penance, and of the example and character of our Divine Lord in His active life, they will seem to survey the reaches of a great river from some height, where the breadth, depth, and fulness of the stream can be seen at a glance.

But the exhibition of the moral and spiritual significance of Christianity is to be seen in its fulness and maturity nowhere as in the mystical theology of the Catholic Church. First of all in the devotions of which the Incarnation is the object, as, for instance, in the devotion of the Holy Name of Jesus, of which S. Bernard, and S. Bernardine of Sienna, the B. John Colombini, and S. Ignatius are the four chief fountains.

Next in the devotion of the Blessed Sacrament in all its forms and manifestations, of which S. Anselm, and S. Bonaventure, and S. Thomas are luminous examples, in the midst of a cloud of saints and servants of God, who by their lives, their preaching, and their writings, have exhibited the mind and delineated the character of Jesus, both as God and man, with a fulness, vividness, tenderness, intimacy and truth, to which no uncatholic writer upon record, in any age of the world, has ever approached so much as afar off.

Again, in the devotion of the Sacred Heart, which is emphatically and articulately the expression of that aspect of the Incarnation and of the Blessed Sacrament which exhibits the mind and character, the personal love and personal relation of our Divine Lord to us, and ours to Him again. From S. Augustine to the Blessed Margaret Mary, there is an unbroken line of saints and writers who not only exhibit this personal aspect of our Saviour to us, but who are witnesses of what the Church, all through those centuries, was teaching to its children. From the time of the Blessed Margaret Mary to this day, the multitude of writers who have brought out this moral and spiritual idea of the Incarnation is literally almost without number. There is hardly a spiritual writer who has not treated or touched upon it. There is not a manual of devotion or a book of prayer in which it is not prominently set forth.

Moreover, every year by the festivals of the Holy Name, the Blessed Sacrament, and of the Sacred Heart, this spiritual teaching is made perpetual and universal.

It is beyond my present purpose to do more than mention the Devotions of the Crucifix, of the Five Sacred Wounds, of the Passion, of the Most Precious Blood, with all the feasts and practices of mental prayer founded upon them. What are these but the most vivid and intimate delineations of the mind and character of our Divine Redeemer?

Lastly, for I cannot here pursue the subject, let any one with the least claim to be a scholar examine the four families of mystical writers, saints, and theologians, which, like the four rivers of Paradise, water the Church of God; namely, the Benedictine, the Dominican, the Franciscan, and the Jesuit; especially the last, in its innumerable works on the Spiritual Exercises of S. Ignatius; and if he be a competent scholar and a candid man, I am confident that he will acknowledge first, that no communion or body separated from the Catholic and Roman Church has ever produced any exhibition of the mind and character of Jesus, or of the moral and spiritual idea of Christianity, I will not say equal in proportion or in fulness, but so much as like in kind, to the mystical theology which, traceably from the fifth century to the nineteenth, has watered the Church of God. The words of the psalmist may be truly said of this stream of the waters of life, ever full and overflowing its banks — 'fluminis impetus lætificat civitatem Dei.' And next, he will be constrained to confess that all this exuberance of the interior spiritual life has diffused itself throughout the Church under the direction of the most rigorous and inflexible dogmatic theology, which has hung suspended with all its constellations of truths over the surface of this inundation of spiritual life, like the firmament over the sea. Certainly dogmatic theology does not treat of the interior life either of the Head or the members of the Church; but it generates the piety and the prayer which sanctifies the soul through the truth, and the mystical theology which directs and sustains it.

Thus much I have thought it necessary to say, in order to anticipate the objection that the tradition of dogma is a tradition of dry and lifeless formulas; and to show that while dogmatic theology is progressive in all the secondary operations of deduction and definition, it is fixed and permanent in all the primary dogmas which express the eternal and immutable order of Divine truths and facts. In all the expansion and advancing analysis of theological science it never parts from its base. It reposes immutably upon the foundation of divine truths and facts, which being divine, are changeless.

To what has been hitherto advanced, I will only add one general conclusion. Unless all that I have said be false, then the accusation against the Catholic doctrines as corruptions, and innovations, as dry, lifeless, transient formulas, cannot by the necessity of the case be true. If God had so given and left His revelation, that the custody of it depends upon the intellect and the will of man, wounded as both are by sin, then corruptions, changes, and innovations would be not only inevitable, but the law of its transmission. But this is contrary not only to the divine procedure and perfections, but to the explicit terms of the revelation itself. God has declared Himself to be, not only the Giver, but the Guardian of His own truth; not only the Promulgator, but the Perpetuator of the light of Pentecost. Now it is this which is denied, when the Catholic doctrines are denounced as corrupt, and the dogma of faith as out of date. It is, as I said, no question of detail, but of the whole Christian dispensation. Either God the Holy Ghost inhabits the Church for ever, and His unction full and perfect, which 'is truth and no lie,' that is the whole truth unmixed and pure, is with the

Church at this hour, or it is not. If He be not with it, and if that unction does not abide with it, then its doctrines may be as corrupt, as novel, as distorted, as lifeless, as arbitrary as the perversity of the intellect and will of man can make them. The line of heresies from Gnosticism to Protestantism are example and proof.

But if He still abide in the Church as its Divine Teacher and Guide, then it follows beyond all controversy that the doctrines of the Church are His utterances, and that in all ages they abide as the radiance of His presence, incorrupt, incorruptible, immutable, and primitive, as on the day when He descended on His apostles. And the words of God by the prophet are fulfilled in Jesus the Head, and in the Church His body: 'My Spirit that is in thee, and my words that I have put in thy mouth, shall not depart out of thy mouth, nor out of the mouth of thy seed, nor out of the mouth of thy seed's seed, saith the Lord, from henceforth and for ever;'[1] that is, of the Holy Catholic and Roman Church, and of the Vicar of the Incarnate Word on earth.

[1] Isaias lix. 21.

www.ingramcontent.com/pod-product-compliance
Lightning Source LLC
Chambersburg PA
CBHW031937230426
43672CB00010B/1951